Nine Medieval
Romances of Magic

Nine Medieval Romances of Magic

Re-Rhymed in Modern English

by Marijane Osborn

broadview press

Library and Archives Canada Cataloguing in Publication

           Nine medieval romances of magic / re-rhymed in modern English by Marijane Osborn.

Includes bibliographical references and index.
ISBN 978-1-55111-997-7

           1. English poetry — Middle English, 1100-1500 — Modernized versions. 2. Romances, English. I. Osborn, Marijane

PR2064.N55 2010   821'.108   C2009-906689-0

Broadview Press is an independent, international publishing house, incorporated in 1985. Broadview believes in shared ownership, both with its employees and with the general public; since the year 2000 Broadview shares have traded publicly on the Toronto Venture Exchange under the symbol bdp.

North America	UK, Europe, Central Asia, Middle East, Africa, India and Southeast Asia
Post Office Box 1243,	
Peterborough, Ontario, Canada K9J 7H5	Eurospan Group
	3 Henrietta St., London, WC2E 8LU, UK
2215 Kenmore Ave.	tel: 44 (0) 1767 604972; fax: 44 (0) 1767 601640
Buffalo, New York, USA 14207	eurospan@turpin-distribution.com
tel: (705) 743-8990; fax: (705) 743-8353	Australia and New Zealand
	NewSouth Books
customerservice@broadviewpress.com	c/o TL Distribution, 15-23 Helles Ave.,
	Moorebank, nsw, Australia 2170
	tel: (02) 8778 9999 ; fax (02) 8778 9944
	orders@tldistribution.com.au

We welcome comments and suggestions regarding any aspect of our publications — please feel free to contact us at the addresses above or at: broadview@broadviewpress.com / www.broadviewpress.com.

Copy-edited by Martin Boyne.

Cover design by Michel Vrana; interior design by Jennifer Blais, Black Eye Design.

Printed in Canada

For Kathleen and Hildy
and all the others who have stood by my PhDs
throughout the hard years of their quest

CONTENTS

ACKNOWLEDGEMENTS

M y first debt pertinent to any project of retelling stories must be
to my mother, Idella Purnell (later Stone), who set me on the
particular path that has led to this book. The stories she read
to us children included the expected European tales of fairies and magic
and Kipling's tales of magical India, but she also read us her own retellings
of tales of magic from less familiar cultures, especially from the native cul-
tures of Mexico. Her two books that I loved most were *The Wishing Owl:
A Maya Story Book* (New York: Macmillan, 1931) and *The Talking Bird: An
Aztec Story Book* (New York: Macmillan, 1944). But she took us to worlds
of the imagination far beyond Mexico. For an example related (distantly) to
this book, in a Kiplingesque poem titled "Strange Harbors," telling of the
US Army experiment of bringing camels to rough-and-ready California,
my mother evoked the more elegant home these "Saracen" animals longed
for. She also encouraged me from a very early age to write poetry of my
own—and, less exaltedly, to rhyme for fun.

When I was myself a young mother, my mother took the children for
the summer and arranged for me to study at the University of Guadalajara,

where Juan Marco Hahn introduced me to Nahuatl poetry and philosophy, and other elements of the culture of the Mexican stories I knew. Thereby he catapulted me into the strange world of scholarship, where I have been held in thralldom ever since.

The third most important person behind this book is Alain Renoir, who drew me into Middle English and made me his teaching assistant when I was still an undergraduate. He had enormous faith in me and remained a mentor over the years until his recent death. Later, when I was a graduate student, Prince William of Gloucester and I became friends on the basis of stories we had read and loved as children, and we remained warm friends until his death. No one else was ever such a "story-friend" to me as William. (And he had the ruins of a haunted castle in his garden.)

I am indebted to others in a different way from those four above. Among these others are the undergraduate students for whom I originally began re-rhyming these romances, so that they could easily read more than there was time for with a syllabus entirely of works in Middle English; my graduate students who have taken some of "my" romances into their own work, especially Yvette Kisor; and Roy Liuzza, who encouraged me to submit these stories for publication. At this point I would like to thank the copy-editor of this book, Martin Boyne, for his meticulous attention to detail and his good-natured patience, Jon Wild for help with the music notation for "Tam Lin," and Tara Lowes for holding the project together. I am also grateful to the University of Illinois Press, the publishers of *Romancing the Goddess*, for permission to include a revised version of "Emaré" in this collection.

Finally, one must remember with gratitude the original tellers of these nine rhymed romances: John Gower, Geoffrey Chaucer, Marie de France, Thomas Chestre, and others whose names are now lost. The pleasure they take, sometimes amused, in their telling of popular stories ripples through these romances and speaks to us across the centuries.

INTRODUCTION

What is a medieval romance? To borrow a simile from Chaucer, scholars "murmur" in defining this genre "as doth a swarm of bees," and because the genre branches out in so many different directions, there are as many complex opinions as there are heads thinking about the problem.[1] Typically, a medieval romance involves a young and noble protagonist, usually male but occasionally female, who travels voluntarily, or is sent away or abducted, from a familiar place into somewhere dangerous and foreign. When on a mission or quest of some kind, the protagonist achieves the quest amid thrilling life-threatening adventures; when abducted or otherwise endangered, he or she escapes with help that may be supernatural. Making it back into a comfort zone at last, the hero of the

---

[1] "The Squire's Tale," lines 202–04. All references to Chaucer's *Canterbury Tales* are to *The Canterbury Tales Complete*, ed. Larry D. Benson (Boston: Houghton Mifflin Co., 2000); tales are quoted by section within the *Tales* followed by line numbers (occasionally by title and line numbers). For a recent overview of attempts to define medieval romance, see K.S. Whetter, *Understanding Genre and Medieval Romance* (Aldershot, UK: Ashgate, 2008), chapter 2.

romance settles there with a life-companion who may have been met along the way, often gaining a kingdom. Although the huge and finally tragic romance of King Arthur and his knights defies this definition in almost every possible way, as does that most "romantic" of medieval tales, the story of the fated lovers Tristan and Isolde, the nine short romances collected here follow this standard pattern of "ease-anxiety-joy."[2]

Naming Tristan and Isolde introduces the issue of the "romantic" love that is associated today with the word "romance." The author of a recent genre study makes love one of the defining elements of medieval English romance: "Whatever other features may commonly occur, the essential and defining features of English romance are the combination and interaction of love and ladies and adventure, culminating in a happy ending" (Whetter 7); he is clearly referring to romantic love. Unlike the French romances by Marie de France called *lais* (in English "lays") and others, however, and wholly unlike the adulterous story of Tristan and Isolde, romances in English, even when their sources are French, tend to feature and support married love or love between persons clearly destined for marriage or its equivalent. Chaucer's romance that he labels a Breton lay, "The Franklin's Tale," addresses this issue specifically. Although romantic love is often a pleasant peripheral issue and part of the joyous outcome, it is rarely a central theme in English romances. More often seriously at stake are power, property, ethics, and concern for worthy achievement, with the notion of personal merit especially marked in the "magical" romances that may involve the training or penance of a knight. Of the nine romances in this book, only the last, "Floris and Blancheflour," is driven primarily by romantic passion—and it is perhaps the least "English" of them all. What marks all nine, however, is the magic that drives, complicates, or resolves the plot.

The Middle English tales of this anthology are mainly of the early fourteenth century to the mid-fifteenth century, with "Floris and Blancheflour" earlier. The first five stories all contain some kind of encounter with fairies or enchantment, and the other four engage "Saracens" and magic; the parodic "Tale of Sir Thopas" contains reference to both. The fairies and elves of these romances are by no means cute little winged creatures. They closely resemble human beings but are usually frightening, or at least intimidating; seeing them dancing in the night makes our hearts rebound "at once with joy and fear" (Milton, *Paradise Lost*, I, 788), and

---

2   The same conventional pattern is followed by the eighteenth-century Gothic novel and the modern formulaic romance novel. As Northrop Frye says, casting his net over romance in general: "Most romances exhibit a cyclical movement of descent into a night world and a return to the idyllic world, or to some symbol of it like a marriage" (*The Secular Scripture: A Study of the Structure of Romance* [Cambridge, MA: Harvard UP], 54).

they have enhanced powers. C.S. Lewis calls such beings the *Longaevi* and has a very readable chapter about them in his book *The Discarded Image*;[3] Tolkien reinvented them for *The Lord of the Rings*. The particular fairies in the romances in this book are all High Fairies (Lewis's term), fairies emanating power like Galadriel.[4] Here, they are shape-shifters or cause others to change shape, or they abduct humans to another realm.

Possibly the magical tale most specific to the late medieval period is that of the shape-shifting "Loathly Lady," who changes from ugly (loathsome) to beautiful, and the changes played upon this theme even today are numerous and fascinating.[5] Only two Loathly Lady tales are included here, but they have an interesting relationship in that the one appears to be at least partly a response to the other; in Gower's tale the Loathly Lady is the traditional victim of an enchantment, whereas in Chaucer's tale the Lady is a fairy with power over her shape, a voluntary shape-shifter. This issue of female agency (or lack thereof) is of paramount interest and seems to lie behind the other contrasting details that Chaucer introduces.[6] Stories of the fairy-abduction type are familiar from Keats's haunting poem "La Belle Dame Sans Merci" (The Beautiful Lady without Mercy),[7] and one of the peculiar things about them is the frequency with which abduction or sexual predation takes place under trees or at the edge of a forest, both liminal sites.[8] In these tales trees seem to function as portals between our known and controllable human realm and the wild spaces beyond. Tales 3, 4, and with a twist, 5, are fairy-abduction tales.

---

[3]   Cambridge: Cambridge UP (Canto), 1964: 122–38.

[4]   In this medieval context of the *Longaevi*, there is no distinction between fairies and elves; the wings and prettiness that distinguish fairies are introduced at a later date.

[5]   The screenplay authors of the film *Shrek* add this medieval theme to their story; it is not in their source, a picture book by William Steig.

[6]   That Chaucer is consciously writing against his friend Gower's tale is not a new idea. Carl Lindahl, for example, suggests that "as Chaucer and Gower almost certainly knew each other's poems, it is entirely possible that the Wife of Bath's Tale was intended as a playful inversion of, and a festive response to the sober clerical cast of Gower's tale" ("The Oral Undertones of Late Medieval Romance," *Oral Tradition in the Middle Ages*, ed. W.F.H. Nicolaisen [New York: Medieval & Renaissance Texts & Studies, 1995], 75). For further discussions of Gower's tale preceding Chaucer's, see n.5 in the introduction to "The Tale of Florent" and also n.5 in the introduction to "The Wife of Bath's Tale."

[7]   The poem was first published in Leigh Hunt's *Indicator* for 10 May 1820, with an introduction by Hunt. He claims that the poem is directly indebted to a medieval poem by Alain Chartier (c. 1390–c. 1430) that Keats would have assumed was by Chaucer; see Edmund Blunden's note on the poem in his edition, *John Keats: Selected Poems* (London: Collins, 1955), 360.

[8]   In Keats's poem the knight wakes up "on the cold hillside" at the edge of a lake. Chaucer recognizes this feature of liminality near the beginning of "The Wife of Bath's Tale"; see lines III 879–81. Later his Loathly Lady appears after a fairy dance "under a forest side" (III 990).

Saracens, the great Eastern antagonists of the Crusaders, are also denizens of a realm beyond what is commonly known, and tales 6 to 9 all refer to Saracens, each in a different way. In general, English romances represent these people as racially alien, occasionally commenting on their skin color,[9] but in romance as well as in real life they were most significantly alien in terms of doctrine. Their Muslim religion made them the token human enemy of medieval Christianity, and thus they appear in the earlier French epics. In the Christian world of English romance, however, being non-Christian often makes a Saracen functionally other than human and therefore adaptable as a powerful "empty signifier that the author can use to denote whatever he or she wishes."[10] Thus the Saracens appearing in this book have nothing to do with Middle Eastern history or religion except in name,[11] and little to do with race. They are as fanciful as fairies and portrayed as sexual predators, giant antagonists that are scarcely human at all, or, with some historical accuracy, as artificers or users of wondrous, admirable objects.[12] As "Sir Thopas" demonstrates, there is an overlap in the English medieval romance genre between fairies, giants, and Saracens. All are alien, uncanny—as are their lands. In order intentionally to enter either the land of the fairies or the mysterious East, it usually appears necessary

---

[9] Usually Saracens are simply described as blue or black when color is an issue, but the skin color of the half-Saracen Feirefiz in Wolfram von Eschenbach's *Parzival* (Percival) is described as partly black and partly white because his parents were of different races. Exactly what this means in terms of his appearance is unclear, but pied (like a magpie) comes to mind.

[10] Lynn Tarte Ramey, *Christian, Saracen and Genre in Medieval French Literature* (New York: Routledge, 2001), 15. Here Ramey is speaking of Saracens specifically in French romance, but the same holds true in all medieval romance. Elsewhere she says, "The Saracen was remarkable above all for his or her ability to transform into whatever literary device the Christian author most needed. If a hideous renegade was called for, a Saracen fit the role. If a model of courtliness and chivalry was on the menu, the Saracen filled the part superbly" (44). They are a wild card of the romance genre that may be played in any number of ways, but nevertheless in traditional ways whether for good or ill. Ramey is concerned especially with the way the image of the Saracen in French epic, in which Saracens are always seen in the context of warfare (37), is modified as the genre transmutes into later French romance (often the basis of English romance), where the role becomes more fluid. Of course a really good Saracen is necessarily a converted Saracen. For a brief overview of the development of the romance genre in English, see Helen Cooper, *The English Romance in Time: Transforming Motifs from Geoffrey of Monmouth to the Death of Shakespeare* (Oxford: Oxford UP, 2004), 22–40.

[11] The name, *sarakenos* in Greek, apparently referred originally to invaders on the Greek borders, then was extended to include Bedouins, and then to cover all persons from the Arabian peninsula and beyond.

[12] Saracens and Jews were associated with the manufacture of intricate metal artifacts, and Muslims in particular with scientific devices from clockwork automatons to astrolabes. Because both types of device depended on principles not generally understood in the West, they were often regarded by Europeans as magical.

to go in disguise or to take on an assumed identity, to be other than oneself. King Orfeo disguises himself as a lowly bard (as does Nicolette in the French romance of *Aucassin and Nicolette*), and to enter the anti-paradise of Babylon Floris pretends to be a merchant, an architect, and finally a flower.

With about a hundred extant romances written in England between 1150 and 1500, not including those now fragmentary or reported lost, many other types of romance exist besides these having fantasy antagonists. Other types include long romances in prose and the great cycle of romances developed around King Arthur and his court, and romances about individual knights associated with the great king, especially Tristan of Cornwall and Arthur's nephew Sir Gawain. Thematically, the long and complex alliterative romance of *Sir Gawain and the Green Knight* belongs in this book; the knight challenger is green because he was enchanted by the most famous fairy of them all, Morgan le Faye—"the fairy." There are romances associated with historical events, like the Charlemagne romances with their Saracen antagonists (though these romances are far from historically accurate), and those associated with pseudo-history, like Chaucer's "Troilus and Criseyde," set during the Trojan War. There are "charter" romances that lay claim to a place by a particular family or group through the exploits of a founding hero; romances where the hero commits a crime that he must expiate to discover a better self; and several romances focused on an innocent woman set adrift. Of course there are also the chivalric romances with the staple theme of the knight who rescues the fair lady. Appendix A offers a passage, from near the end of a very long romance, where the kiss of a young rescuer knight disenchants a dragon with a woman's face (another disturbing Loathly Lady). To his great astonishment and further dismay, on being disenchanted she stands before him stark naked. Such wealth of theme and mood and variety of length offers much to choose from, so the choice for this anthology of relatively short romances in verse with the fantasy theme of the alien Other should not be considered representative of medieval romance in general, but merely of one small and attractive area of this vast resource.

Why were so many of these stories composed in verse? Perhaps because rhythmic verse is easier to remember than a story in prose. Rhymed romances originated, it is thought, as oral entertainments in the great halls of nobles; a number of them were rather easily worked into ballads in later centuries, and ballads, of course, are intended as song. (See Appendix A for a ballad with its traditional melody.) Sometimes such live entertainment appears within a tale, as when Sir Orfeo plays his harp for the King of the Fairies in order to win back his wife. (This is the ancient story of Orpheus and Eurydice reformulated as an English romance.) The original short romances called "Breton lays" are said to have been sung, and song lyrics are typically in verse, rhythmic and rhymed to go with a repeated melody. But there is another reason for the verse form of these romances that modern silent readers will find hard to believe until they try it. The kind of story encountered here actually moves more quickly than the prose narratives we are used to, because the rhythms, often "galloping" in an unsophisticated way, carry the reader or listener along.[13]

Three types of meter dominate in these romances: rhymed couplets in a loose four-stress meter, "tail-rhyme" stanzas, and Chaucer's iambic pentameter couplets, the new meter. It was not until Chaucer made his imported iambic pentameter (five-stress line) seem natural in English that storytelling in rhymed verse began again to be as sophisticated as some of the adventures formerly told in the native alliterative verse. An interesting transition between the old and new styles of verse romance can be seen in the two Loathly Lady tales told by John Gower and Chaucer that begin this anthology: Gower's "Tale of Florent" is in the older four-stress meter, and Chaucer's "Wife of Bath's Tale" is in iambic pentameter, an innovation at the time but "natural" to us now. When Chaucer's tale is read directly after that by Gower, the difference in feeling is striking. In his "Tale of Sir Thopas" Chaucer parodies the naïve nature of the tail-rhyme stanza, an extremely popular verse-form in the fourteenth century. The stanza is usually made up of four sets of three lines rhyming aax-bbx-ccx-ddx, with x the so-called "tail." The abcd lines are in tetrameter (four beats) and the x or tail-rhyme lines are in trimeter, offering an impression rather like a ballad. It is a "light" rhythm that would be entirely unsuited to the vast romances ending in tragedy. Nevertheless, like the also sing-songy ballad meter, tail-rhyme meter does not preclude affecting moments.

So what is a romance? At least one can say that all the stories in this particular anthology end (or in the case of "Sir Thopas" potentially end) as most of us feel a romance, so closely akin to fairytale, should end, with our hero overcoming great odds to "live happily ever after" with his or her beloved. Perhaps that reassuring conclusion is the most typical aspect of a story, either medieval or modern, with magic or without, that we would normally call a romance today.

---

[13] Such rhythms may also propel the translator. Appendix B discusses the difficulties and delights of translating medieval metrical romance.

CHAPTER I

The Tale of Florent

"The Tale of Florent" by John Gower (1325?–1408) is about a young knight keeping a promise even under threat of death, and how that act, besides demonstrating his commitment to his word of honor, conveys an honorable public identity. In the second part of the story, however, a mysterious and ugly old woman, a "Loathly Lady" in folklore terms, arrives just in time to aid the endangered knight, and entraps him into another contract—this time of a marriage that threatens to besmirch his public identity. Thus Gower's knight Florent pledges his troth, irrevocably, twice: at line 1487, to go on a quest, and at line 1588, to marry the hag. Both of the women who trap him into making these separate vows use the legalized language of "covenant" (lines 1450 and 1590; see also 1636), language to which Florent responds in similar terms (lines 1474–76). The first covenant is tested in a law scene in open court, the second privately. Four of the nine romances in this book include court scenes of judgment and three have scenes with an affinity to these, all of them having something to do with keeping the pledged, or even idly spoken, word.[1]

Many scholars believe that the Loathly Lady plot derives ultimately from a Celtic source.[2] In one familiar Irish tale, several brothers go in turn to fetch water at a well, and the well-guardian, an ugly hag, asks each for love. They are naturally reluctant to comply, but finally one brother agrees to embrace her. As soon as he does so, the hag becomes a beautiful woman and reveals that she is the "Sovereignty of Ireland" and that he will rule the land. In the English Loathly Lady story, versions of which "circulated from the thirteenth century or before,"[3] the sovereignty issue may begin with land tenure; but a riddle-quest is introduced, and the emphasis of the second part of the story in its later form places sovereignty in the domestic realm, between man and wife. The story typically begins with the protagonist, who has committed some kind of crime, being caught and challenged to a riddle to save his neck; in the second part he goes on a quest to find the answer and meets the Loathly Lady, who tells him the solution, at a price. In later versions of this story involving King Arthur (who has wrongly appropriated land), Sir Gawain comes along to help the king find the answer, a well-chosen hero since he is the most courteous to women of all Arthur's knights. The ugly hag appears and gives him the answer to convey to the king to save him, but then Gawain is committed to marrying her. Reluctantly he does so, and then she offers him a final challenge, a choice. When he defers the decision to her, allowing her sovereignty in the matter, she becomes beautiful. Unlike the Irish sovereignty goddess, the hag in the English "Gawain" tales is under an enchantment, usually imposed by the traditional wicked stepmother. So the plot of the story falls into two main parts: first the crime with the riddle quest, then the Loathly Lady's answer,

---

[1] For the importance of understanding "pledging troth" in the context of the crossover period between spoken and written legal contracts, see Richard Firth Green, *A Crisis of Truth: Law and Literature in Ricardian England* (Philadelphia: U of Pennsylvania P, 1999). I am grateful to Alison L. Ganze for contributing to my understanding of this complex issue.

[2] Sigmund Eisner, *A Tale of Wonder: A Source Study of The Wife of Bath's Tale* (Folcroft, PA: Folcroft Press, 1970; rpt. of the 1957 ed.).

[3] Thomas Hahn, "Gawain and Popular Romance in Britain," *The Cambridge Companion to Medieval Romance* (Cambridge UP, 2000), 230. Hahn offers a brief history of the Loathly Lady tale in English romance and situates the versions featuring Gawain in relation to the others (230–33). In an earlier essay, "Old Wives' Tales and Masculine Identities," Hahn describes in some detail the thirteenth-century "Hag's Masque" (as he calls it) in the court of Edward I and then goes on to show how the story in its later forms "frequently serves, for example, as a test for establishing masculine identity according to specific cultural norms" (*Retelling Tales: Essays in Honor of Russell Peck*, ed. Thomas Hahn and Alan Lupack [Cambridge: D.S. Brewer, 1997], 94).

followed by marriage, a new "riddle," and the transformation. Sometimes a magic kiss is involved.

Wherever Gower got the broad folktale outlines of his story, he has changed it to suit his purpose in Book I of the *Confessio Amantis*. This work is a frame-tale in which the young Amans ("lover") is instructed by his mentor Genius, and in Book I, lines 1407–1882, Genius tells the Loathly Lady tale as an exemplary story to teach the young man how to behave properly toward women, which is to say, in a humble, courtly fashion. Gower sets his story in the Welsh borderlands (the most likely interpretation of *marches* at line 1417); this is Arthur country, but Gower does not mention that association. Florent's "crime" is the killing of a knight in battle (he is not a murderer), and when he finds himself taken captive by the knight's family, the plot begins to correspond to other English versions of the Loathly Lady tale. The family does not dare kill Florent outright, because of both his reputation and his relationship to the emperor—he is the emperor's nephew, as Gawain is nephew to King Arthur. So the wily and devious grandmother of the slain knight proposes to use Florent's reputation for honor to trap him with the riddle quest, thinking the answer to her question is impossible for a man to find. She puts Florent on his honor to succumb to punishment if he cannot find it, and he pledges his *trawthe* (troth) accordingly.[4] Gower's story is a close analogue to Chaucer's more famous "Wife of Bath's Tale" and most likely a source for it, since these poets were contemporaries and friends. They apparently had a relationship rather like that between C.S. Lewis and J.R.R. Tolkien, feeding each other ideas with a certain amount of creative rivalry.[5]

The translation below owes much to Russell A. Peck's TEAMS edition of this romance. Subtitles have been added in order to align Gower's

---

[4] At lines 1512, 1559, etc., the word *trawthe* is translated by its cognate word "troth" (as in betrothed), but this medieval word for a pledge has complex implications. See Green for discussion of these implications.

[5] In an important essay that became available to the author when this book was already in press, Russell A. Peck argues persuasively, confirming what is more tentatively proposed here, that the "Tale of Florent," "drawing upon folk material," is "the first sustained Loathly Lady narrative in English Literature," and that rather than Gower's tale and Chaucer's "Wife of Bath's Tale" having a common source now lost, Gower's tale "functioned as the primary source for 'The Wife of Bath's Tale'"—and for the other English Loathly Lady tales that followed. "The subsequent writers, of course, drew upon other materials as well as they reshaped Gower's assemblage for new purposes" ("Folklore and Powerful Women in Gower's 'Tale of Florent,'" *The English "Loathly Lady" Tales: Boundaries, Traditions, Motifs*, ed. S. Elizabeth Passmore and Susan Carter, Studies in Medieval Culture XLVIII [Kalamazoo, MI: Medieval Institute Publications, 2007], 100). Peck's rich and careful assessment is now crucial reading for anyone seeking to understand the history of these stories.

tale with Chaucer's tale that follows, to which similar titles are added, and the line numbers refer to the *Confessio Amantis*. Gower's switching back and forth between tenses, although frowned upon in modern English, has been kept, and his rhymed tetrameter couplet meter, a typical romance meter, is imitated.

The Tale of Florent

Part I: The "Crime" and the Quest

Once there was, in days of old,
A worthy knight who, it is told,
Was nephew to the emperor
1410   And of his court a courtier.
Still wifeless, Florent was his name,
And for his strength he had great fame.
In arms he wanted to excel
In chivalry, in love as well.
1415   To be regarded highly, he
Sought foreign ventures constantly
And through the Marches[6] rode about.

There came a time when he was out
That Fortune,[7] which with ease may pluck
1420   Apart a person's web of luck,
Caused Florent, as he rode along,
To be surrounded by a strong
Army, and to a castle led
Where our Florent few friends had.
1425   For in the battle when they caught
Florent, it happened, as he fought,
That he had dealt a wound that slew
Branchus, who son and heir was to
The Captain.[8] Therefore, full of wrath
1430   Were the father and mother both.

The slain Sir Branchus was the man
Best at fighting in all the land.
His parents would have much preferred
To take revenge, but were deterred
1435   By both the thought of Florent's worth

---

6   Marches: Welsh borderlands.
7   Fortune is imagined here as "lady luck."
8   The Captain: the ruler of the castle.

In knighthood, and his noble birth.[9]
He to the emperor was related
As nephew, so they hesitated,
Fearing reprisal. They did not dare
1440   To slay him, so they argued there
Among themselves: what best to do?

There was a lady, the slyest who
Was known to men, so old that she
Could only walk with difficulty.
1445   She was the grandmother of the dead
Young knight, and to his parents said
That she could reel in Florent yet
And by her wiles contrive to get
The very man himself to grant
1450   His death through strength of covenant;
And none of them would get the blame.
She sent for him, and soon he came.
Of Branchus first she spoke, her dead
Grandson, and then to Florent said:
1455   "You know that you have been the cause
Of Branchus' death. Though we have laws
That give for vengeance clear permission,
We'll let you live on one condition.
Accept, with us to judge, this task:
1460   A simple question I shall ask,
And you must find the answer true.
But also you must swear, if you
Should fail to find the right reply,
No other recourse will you try,
1465   But willingly your death receive.
And so that no one may deceive
You in this, nothing may be changed.
You shall have day and time arranged
To go unharmed, provided that

---

9   Noble birth: *gentilesse*. Lines 1437–38 show that by Middle English *gentilesse* Gower clearly means "high birth." Chaucer's hag disputes this meaning for the word in her lecture on *gentilesse* to the knight in "The Wife of Bath's Tale." The word is often translated as "nobility," which has the same ambiguous meaning in modern English, as it may refer either to rank or to ethics.

1470 You will return, on the day we set,
    To bring your answer. You won't be hurt."

    Astute was Florent and alert.
    He asked the lady to reveal
    And have it written under seal
1475 Exactly for what question he
    Would place his life in jeopardy.
    So then the woman began pretending
    That she thought only of befriending
    Florent, and said, "Oh, it's about
1480 Love, that you'll be finding out—
    What thing all women most desire,
    And then you'll have this whole empire,
    Wherever knowledge is, to seek
    Your answer, then come back here to speak."
1485 Florent agreed to this, and so
    The day was set, the time to go.
    Under his seal he wrote his oath
    In his own way and then went forth
    Home to his uncle's[10] court again.
1490 The tale he told him, short and plain,
    Of his adventure, what befell,
    Which hearing, his uncle sent for all
    The wisest of the land, but none
    Of them could settle on just one
1495 Clear answer, in agreement flat.
    Some said this and others that,
    According to the disposition
    Of their natural complexion[11]—
    For what to one woman gives pleasure
1500 May grieve another without measure.
    But as for one particular
    Thing that all women near and far
    Will find most pleasant and desired
    Above all else ... This they inquired,
1505 But such a thing they could not find
    By horoscopes or any kind

---

[10] Florent's uncle is the emperor.

[11] Complexion: their psychology, referring to the medieval concept of the four "humors" or bodily fluids.

Of thought. So Florent, lacking aid,
Must take his chance of fortune made—
Or likely lost, he thinks, by lack
1510   Of answers—when he must go back.

This noble knight would rather die
Than break his troth and fail thereby
To come back to the place he swore
He would return to. When, therefore,
1515   The time came, he was prompt to say
Farewell, for he could not delay.
He asked that his uncle be not loath
To see him go, since he by oath
Was bound, and that no knight should try
1520   To avenge his honor if he should die,
Whatever afterwards men might say.
Thus Florent went upon his way
Like any lone knight on a quest,
And now he wondered what was best
1525   Under this circumstance to try.

Part II: The Hag

Riding alone, as he drew nigh
The place where he had sworn to be,
In a forest, beneath a tree,
He saw where an ugly creature sat,
1530   A somewhat womanish figure that,
Speaking just of flesh and bone,
Was certainly the ugliest crone
He'd ever seen, and quickly he
Had nearly ridden past, when she
1535   Called out to him and said, "Abide!"
So Florent turned his horse aside
And back to her he rode. Then he
Pulled up and waited there to see
What the woman from him was seeking,
1540   And then to him she started speaking.

She told him: "Florent, by your name,
You've undertaken such a game,

That now, unless you're well advised,
Your death's so certainly devised
1545   That all the world cannot save thee,
Unless you take advice from me."
When Florent heard the woman state
The course so calmly of his fate,
He asked what counsel she could give.
1550   "So, Florent," she said, "you want to live.
If I were to arrange it through
My skill that not only death do you
Escape, but honor gain from it,
What thing should be my benefit?"
1555   "Whatever thing you ask," said he.
"What better payment could there be?"
She said. "But first, before you go,
Give me a pledge, that I may know
I have your troth, in my hand here,
1560   That you shall be my husband dear."
"Ah, no," said Florent, "that may not be."
"Then ride upon your way," said she,
"But if you ride on lacking my
Advice, then you shall surely die!"

1565   In land, in rent, in park, in plough,[12]
Florent promises to endow
Her with great wealth, but that is not
Her wish. Then, deeply into thought,
He rides away, then back to her.
1570   He does not know which to prefer,
For now, as to and fro he goes,
He must choose one of these, he knows:
To take this woman as his wife
Or otherwise to lose his life.
1575   And then he thought her age might be
To his advantage, so old was she,
For he could take her away to hide
Her on an island until she died,
And nobody would ever know
1580   He had such a wife. On thinking so,

---

[12] These are categories of income-producing land.

At last the knight so young and handsome
Came to this loathly hag unwinsome
To say, "If there's no other chance
Of getting my deliverance
1585   Except by that specific speech
That you say only you can teach,
Have here my hand. We shall be wed!"
And thus his word of troth he said.

Upon that word she raised her brow.
1590   "This covenant I will allow,"
She said. "If any other lore[13]
Than what I give suffices for
Saving you from your death, I shall
Acquit you of your troth in all—
1595   But I'm sure there's no other way.
Now listen closely to what I say.
When you have come into the place
Where they anticipate your disgrace
And all wait there impatiently,
1600   This is the way it's going to be:
They'll ask at once for you to give
The answer that will let you live,
Whichever one you think is best.
But let your heart be now at rest.
1605   You need not worry any more.
Just pay attention to my lore.
Every woman who lives, you'll say,
On earth wants things to be this way:
To be the sovereign of a man's love,
1610   For any woman so placed above
Shall have, as one might say, her will;
She cannot her desire fulfill
Otherwise—what she wants the most.
With this one answer to your host
1615   You'll save yourself, no other way.
And when you've thereby saved the day,
Come here again, and you will find
Me waiting. Don't let it slip your mind."

---

[13]   Lore: learning, method.

Forth he goes with heavy heart,
1620   Like one who knows not how to start
To find the joy he might attain,
For if condemned, he endures that pain,
And if he lives, he's pledged to bind
Himself to her who of womankind
1625   Is, more than anyone, ugliest.
He can't imagine what is best.
Like it or not, though, forth he goes
On to the castle where he knows
That with an answer he must reply,
1630   Whether it be to live or die.

Forth with his council came the lord.
He told the court scribe to record
Proceedings, sent for the crone, who came
At once, and told her to proclaim
1635   Before the assembled parliament
The strength of all the covenant.[14]
She now proclaimed it openly,
And then told Florent, whatever he
Had found, it was now time to say,
1640   Well knowing the price he had to pay.
Florent gave first some of his own
Answers that he had found alone
Either by payment or by gift,
The sentence of his death to lift.
1645   Thus long and late did Florent tarry,
Until the lady said to hurry,
That for the final judgment he
Must answer the question specifically
That she so long ago had posed.
1650   So when he finally supposed
That he had nothing else to give
Of answers that might let him live
Except what that old hag had taught,
From that a little hope he got
1655   That he might be excused. Therefore
Now he uttered the old hag's lore.

---

[14] This is the second time this significant term, "strength of covenant," is used; see line 1450
and the introduction to the story, above.

And when this thing the Matron heard,
How he had answered word for word,
"Hah, treason! Woe to you!" said she,
1660   "And who has told you secretly
What thing all women most desire?
I wish you could be set on fire!"[15]
Nevertheless, by this correct
Answer did Florent save his neck.

Part III: Keeping Trouthe

1665   But then began his sorrow anew,
For he must go—or be untrue—
To her to whom he pledged his troth.
So dreading shame and lying both,[16]
He goes to where he's meeting her,
1670   Planning his penance to endure
Like one who was with troth affaited.[17]
And this old woman for him has waited
Where he left her beneath the tree.
He lifted his drooping head to see
1675   This hag, this horror, where she sat.
She was the loathsomest creature that
Ever a man cast eye upon.
Her eyebrows went up, her nose went down,
Her eyes were small and deeply set,
1680   Her cheeks with slimy tears were wet

---

[15] Set on fire: i.e., burnt at the stake.

[16] He fears shame if he marries the hag, lying if he does not honor his "troth" (line 1667). This idea that breaking a vow (*trouthe*) is equivalent to a lie is found also in Chaucer's "Merchant's Tale" (IV 2311–15).

[17] The French word *affaited* (in the original text) has a complex nuance here. The editors translate it as *governed*, and *Cassell's French-English, English-French Dictionary* agrees: *affaiter* "to train (hawks)." But in addition to this meaning, the Stratmann-Bradley *Middle-English Dictionary* gives *adorned, fitted, shaped*, and *Cassell's* also adds "to dress (leather)." In my understanding, then, this word raises questions of identity formation: Florent, as a knight laying claim to nobility (in both senses here), can do nothing else but keep the pledge that he has previously voiced. To say it is to do it, indeed to be it (see lines 1666, 1668, 1700–02, 1715–16). Florent's anxiety about lying at line 1666 is emphasized above for the rhyme with "both," but also because lying is linked with *untrowthe* elsewhere. The meaning of *trouthe*, narrowly translated here as "troth," is also linked with notions of truth and identity as well as with the idea of a pledge (as in "betrothal").

And wrinkled as an empty skin,[18]
And hanging down upon her chin.
Her lips were shrunken in her face,
And in her visage was no grace.

1685 With forehead narrow, through hair gone white,
She peered as a Moorish woman might.[19]
Her shoulders bent around her bust
In a way disturbing to manly lust;
Her body was huge and far from slim,

1690 And to describe her in brief, no limb
Was there without deficiency,
And like some bulging wool-sack, she
Proffers herself, and tells him now
It's time for him to honor his vow

1695 And keep his covenant with her,
Because she's been his guarantor.
By the bridle she seizes him,
But God knows if she pleases him
By the hard words she is speaking.

1700 Florent thinks his heart is breaking
Because he knows he must not flee
Unless untrue he wants to be.

You know how, seeking wellness, one
Takes gentian root with cinnamon

1705 To get the sweetness with the myrrh?[20]
In this way Florent might prefer
To mix his sorrow in this diet:
Bitter with sweet, he has to try it,
So mingles sorrow with delight

1710 And lives while dying (as one might
Perceive it), casting away his youth
Upon a woman who is, in truth,
As old and ugly as is she.
He must endure what needs to be,

1715 And to his troth he will be true,
As any loyal knight must do,
Whatever might to him befall,

---

18 Skin: i.e., wineskin, which wrinkles up when empty.

19 Presumably as a Muslim woman looks out from her hijab or veil.

20 Myrrh: a bitter herb, here representing bitterness itself.

Though she's the ugliest of them all.
Yet to the honor of womanhood
1720 It seemed to Florent that he should
Take heed, and so with gentleness
He raised her in her tattered dress
(Her clothing was all torn and coarse)
And set her before him on his horse,
1725 And forth he gently takes his way.

No wonder he does not ride by day;
No wonder he often heaves a sigh,
And as in darkness an owl will fly[21]
When other birds can have no sight
1730 Of him, throughout the day this knight
Kept hidden, and arranged to ride
By night to where he would abide.
When he arrived, without ado,
In secret he brought this creature to
1735 His castle now in such a wise
That nobody could see her guise
Until she came into his room.
Into his counsel he took those whom
He most among his friends could trust,
1740 Explaining to them why he must
Take this foul woman as his wife:
How he'd have otherwise lost his life.

And then he privately ordered brought
Some women he was sure would not
1745 Gossip, and her rags they very
Gently drew off. As customary,
She had a bath then, and a rest,
And then was elegantly dressed.
But no comb had the power to
1750 Smooth out her tangles or go through
That hair, nor would she let them cut
Any of it off, no matter what.
So then their cleverness they used

---

21   The specificity of this owl simile, found also in Chaucer's "Wife of Bath's Tale" in a similar context (at line 1081 of that tale), is evidence that one of these stories is a response to the other.

(Deciding that it was excused)
1755   To hide her defects craftily
In hopes that nobody could see.
But when in fine clothes she was decked
And her attire was duly checked,
Uglier than before was she.
1760   But otherwise it could not be,
So they were married in the night.

More woebegone was never a knight
As Florent on his wedding day.
She flirted with him as if to say,
1765   "I'm good enough for anyone!"
But he was getting nothing done,
So she took over, said that he
Was now her husband, and told him, "We
Should now, my lord, get into bed,
1770   Because I for this purpose wed:
That you would be my worldly bliss."[22]
With that she proffered him a kiss
Just as if she attractive were.
His body then might be with her,
1775   But as for thought and memory,
His heart was off in purgatory.
Yet matrimony has its laws.
He must take pains and try, because
No more excuse can he make that he
1780   Is there in bed for the company.

Conclusion

Later when naked they lay in bed,[23]
Sleeplessly he was tormented.
He turned upon his other side
Because he so desired to hide
1785   His eyes from looking at that wight[24]
In the bed-chamber full of light

---

[22] This is persuasive but not precisely true; see what she says later at lines 1846–49.

[23] They have apparently had sex; see line 1793 below.

[24] Wight: person.

Shining through curtains of sendal[25] thin.
And now the bride who lay within
Had turned to put, to his alarm,
1790 Gently around her lord her arm
And, since he'd turned away, began
To urge him to turn back again.
"For now," she said, "we two are one."
But there he lay as still as stone.
1795 She went on speaking, and she bade
Him think of the promise that he made
The day he pledged her[26] with his hand.
Then he began to understand
Fully the penance he must endure.
1800 Like someone in a trance, toward her
He turned around—and to his view
Appeared a lady beside him who
Was eighteen years of age, he guessed,
And her face was the loveliest
1805 That ever in all the world there'd been.
He would have pulled her closer then,
But with a "by your leave," she thrust
Her hand to stop him! First he must,
She told him, one of two things choose,
1810 Whether it was to win or lose:
To have her lovely just at night,
Or have her beautiful by the light
Of day, for he could not have both.
Then he began to grieve, for loath
1815 He was to choose, and much he thought,
But for all that, he just could not
Make a decision which was best.
She wanted to set his heart at rest,
But still she said he must decide.
1820 At last he said, "Tell me, my bride,
The one that you, my life's salvation,
Prefer in this deliberation.
I do not know what I should do.
I want, as long as I live, for you

---

25 Sendal: a silky fabric.
26 Pledged her: i.e., at line 1587.

1825   To be my mistress,[27] and which is best
    For my own good, I cannot guess—
    Which answer is the better choice.
    Therefore I grant you my whole voice,[28]
    So choose for both of us, I pray,
1830   As you prefer. Whichever you say,
    Just as you wish it, so do I."

    "My lord," she said, "I thank you. By
    Those words that you have said to me,
    You've given me full sovereignty,
1835   And thus my destiny I fulfill.
    Never again diminished will
    The beauty be that now I have.
    Until I'm taken to my grave,
    I'll always be, by night and day,
1840   The same to you, and look this way.
    The king's daughter of Sicily
    I am, and when I recently
    Was with my father, it befell
    That my stepmother put a spell
1845   (Because she hated me) upon
    My beauty, lasting till I won
    Love and sovereignty from a knight
    Who in his reputation right
    Above all others stood—and see:
1850   It is apparent that you are he,
    As proven by your deed.[29] Therefore
    I shall be yours forevermore."

    Then great was the pleasure and joy as they
    Together began to laugh and play,
1855   And long they lived and well endured,
    And clerks that this adventure heard
    Have written it as evidence,

---

[27] Clarification may be useful here. The text says *maistresse*, from which we get the word "mistress." Florent, however, refers to mastery, not an illicit partner in sexual activity as the modern word implies. He means that he wants her to be his partner in life and have the controlling hand.

[28] Voice: authority to decide.

[29] Deed: i.e., he kept his troth. (Her language still sounds legalistic rather than amorous.)

> To teach us how obedience
> To ladies leads to luck in love,
> 1860   To sit in joy and bliss above,[30]
> Just as it happened to this knight.
>
> Therefore, my son,[31] to do it right,
> Your lady-love you must obey
> And follow her will in every way.

---

[30] To sit in joy and bliss above: Gower is referring to the popular medieval concept of the Wheel of Fortune, where a person riding at the top of the wheel knows happiness.

[31] "Son" here is a term of affection, not relationship. In this conclusion that breaks us so suddenly out of the world of Florent, Genius, the teacher and storyteller in the frame tale of the *Confessio Amantis*, wraps up his story with a moral about appropriate behavior for a lover. It is directed specifically at Amans (the lover), who is his immediate audience.

CHAPTER 2

The Wife of Bath's Tale

Like Gower's "Tale of Florent," this romance, the most famous of Chaucer's *Canterbury Tales*, combines two main folktale themes: the knight's quest for the riddle-answer that will save his life, and the transformation of a "Loathly Lady" into a lovely young woman. Many versions of the riddle-plus-transformation story exist, but only Chaucer combines the two themes in a way that makes the riddle itself thematic, and he does this by making some radical changes to the story.[1] The following paragraph focuses on only two.

Perhaps the most dramatic of all Chaucer's changes is beginning the action of "The Wife of Bath's Tale" with a rape. This is radically different from any of the analogues of the story, especially those with two protagonists of which the main one is Sir Gawain, the most courteous

---

[1]   See the introduction to "Florent" in Chapter One for discussion of how traditional this story actually is, with some discussion of its earlier analogues. It seems likely now that Chaucer is retelling the story from Gower's version.

toward women of all the knights of the Round Table.[2] Both Gower and Chaucer maintain a single protagonist throughout the story, but Gower's young knight is virtuous, whereas Chaucer's protagonist, utterly unlike either Florent or Gawain, is vile toward women.[3] By having the story begin with a rape, Chaucer makes the riddle question about women's desire pertinent to the knight's re-education and, according to the story, redemption. Chaucer's other major change is to put fairies in the story. Having allowed the Wife of Bath to introduce the idea of fairies, their dance, and their queen, Chaucer then changes the Loathly Lady from an enchanted maiden, dependent on a man for her release, to the Fairy Queen herself,[4] a woman upon whom the man depends even more than he realizes—for *his* transformation, a moral one. In this story the Loathly Lady has agency over her shape, and this significantly changes her relationship to the protagonist, as well as being a thematic contrast to the maiden's powerlessness in the initial rape. "Sovereignty" becomes thereby a concern with body and marriage, rather than rule over an area of land.

Class is also an issue. In keeping with the Wife of Bath's identity, the hag's long lecture on good behavior makes a Gawain-like courtesy toward persons of all ranks and genders, whereas Gower focuses on "trawthe"

---

[2]   Gawain is never responsible for the crime with which the story begins in later versions, and at the end of the romance his deference to the ugly old lady releases her from her enchantment. Chaucer refers to his traditional politeness without irony in "The Squire's Tale," line 95: "Gawayn with his olde curteisye."

[3]   This feature entirely changes the nature of the romance: rather than being about a good man being tricked but holding firm, Chaucer's story is about a bad man being redeemed. Carl Lindahl, who examines differences between Gower's and Chaucer's stories, points out a double role reversal involving Chaucer's knight: "Neither a warrior nor a faithful servant [like Florent], he is rather a rapist spared execution by Arthur solely through the intervention of Guenever and her court of ladies (This is an exact role reversal of the power relations in *Florent*, where the faultless knight is unfairly tried by a criminal woman.)" ("The Oral Undertones of Late Medieval Romance," *Oral Tradition in the Middle Ages*, ed. W.F.H. Nicolaisen [New York: Medieval & Renaissance Texts & Studies, 1995], 73).

[4]   As everyone knows who has ever had a childhood, fairies are skittish: now you see them, now you don't, and Chaucer reproduces that magical elusiveness in his tale a little too successfully for some readers. (To spell out blatantly how he does it is something of a spoiler in terms of Chaucer's plot, so a first-time reader might wish to stop reading this note now.) As mentioned above, first Chaucer introduces the "elf-queene" dancing with her maidens (lines 860–61). The fairy dance is a standard feature of English fairy lore extant even today in the "occult" explanation of crop circles. In the story the protagonist actually sees this dance (lines 990–92), which naturally vanishes as he approaches (with curiosity, not lust), leaving only the hag—whose identity we, but not he, should recognize despite her assumed shape. Later she claims that she could "amend" her age and ugliness if she wants (lines 1097 and 1106) and might do this on one condition (line 1108). When the knight fulfills that condition (line 1231), she transforms herself again (line 1249). Chaucer has given us a Loathly Lady different in *species* from the human maiden victimized by an enchanter and dependent on a man's deference or kiss to be saved.

among the highborn. Thus the identity of the teller herself (as well as Chaucer's revision of the story's characters) reflects upon the tale. Every story ever told is situated by its context, and in this case we are told what the context is: the Wife of Bath is telling the tale. This makes the tale part of a larger story. In her confessional prologue in *The Canterbury Tales*, the Wife, now over forty, remembers her amorous youth and beauty, and concludes by telling us about her brutal marriage to a younger man whom she loves; thereby the happier tale that Chaucer has her tell becomes a sort of wish fulfillment for the aging Wife, though she reverts to her feisty "I don't care" attitude right at the end.

It is thought that Chaucer wrote "The Wife of Bath's Tale" in the early 1390s, substituting it for another tale that he had previously assigned to the Wife (most likely "The Shipman's Tale"). It is possible that by mentioning Bretons in the second line, Chaucer intends us to think of his tale as another Breton lay (see the introduction to "Sir Orfeo"), but the verse form is not that of a Breton lay at all. Instead, the story is composed of rhymed couplets in the iambic pentameter that Chaucer himself made viable as a meter for English narrative poetry, and this "new" meter takes some getting used to after reading Gower's tale in the shorter lines typical of medieval romance. In this respect and others, Chaucer seems to have been responding to Gower's version as well as introducing the Arthurian theme when he wrote his own tale.[5]

"The Wife of Bath's Tale" is found in Fragment III (or Group D) of *The Canterbury Tales*. Line numbers in the translation correspond to those in *The Canterbury Tales Complete* (ed. Benson), the text from which the tale is modernized here.[6] Subtitles are added to align the tale with Gower's "Tale of Florent."

---

[5] It has been proposed that Chaucer may have been the one to introduce the Arthurian theme, since there is no evidence that the association of that king with the Loathly Lady theme is traditional before his tale. If this is the case, he may have been led to that idea by geography. Gower omits any reference to King Arthur while locating his tale in the Marches, and this along with the Wife's association with the Bath area may have inspired Chaucer to have her begin her tale with the iconic and magical "King in the West." The idea that Chaucer is responding to "The Tale of Florent" is not new; see n.6 in the Introduction and (especially) n.5 in the introduction to "The Tale of Florent." Also, as John Hurt Fisher says, "If he knew Gower's tale of Constance from Book II of the *Confessio*"—about which there is no argument—"it is hard to imagine that Chaucer did not know Florent from Book I" (*John Gower: Moral Philosopher and Friend of Chaucer* [London: Methuen, 1965], 296).

[6] It is a pleasure to acknowledge here how Peter G. Beidler's very useful anthology of text and articles in *The Wife of Bath* (Boston: Bedford/St. Martin's, 1996), as well as correspondence with its author, has guided the translator's reflections upon this story over the years.

The Wife of Bath's Tale

Part I: The Crime and the Quest

When Arthur was the king in days of old
(He whom the Bretons[7] in great reverence hold),
Entirely filled with fairies was this land.
860   The elf-queen with her jolly elven band
Would often dance in many a meadow green,
Or so they say in old books I have seen.
I speak of centuries past, in days of yore,
But now no one can see them any more,
865   For now the great beneficence and prayers
Of limitors[8] and other holy friars
Who search through every field and every stream
As thick as dust-motes in a sunny beam,
Blessing the halls and chambers, kitchens, bowers,
870   Cities and strongholds, castles and high towers,
Villages, barns and stables, even dairies—
These make it certain that there are no fairies.
Wherever formerly might walk an elf
Now walks the friar mendicant[9] himself,
875   And morn and afternoon, throughout the day,
Says matins and the other things they pray,
And goes through all his district, begging there.
Women may now walk safely everywhere,
For under every bush and every tree
880   There is no other incubus but he,
And he will only do them some dishonor.[10]

One time it so befell that this King Arthur
Had a young bachelor knight there in his court,
And riding along the river, just for sport,
885   He chanced, alone as he was born, to see

---

7   Bretons: inhabitants of Brittany in France.

8   Limitors: friars licensed to beg within a limited district.

9   Mendicant: friar of a begging order.

10   Do them some dishonor: i.e., seduce them. Chaucer (or the Wife of Bath) is being ironic
here. This opening of her story, in which she introduces the theme of fairies, is also intended
to get back at the friar who has recently interrupted her prologue that precedes this tale.

A maiden walking there before him. He
Assaulted her, however much she pled,
And robbed her roughly of her maidenhead.
The knight's oppressive act engendered such
890   An outcry, and the folk complained so much
To Arthur that, invoking law, he said
The knight must die. He would have lost his head
(It happened that this was the statute then),
Except the queen and others, stepping in—
895   All ladies—prayed the king for clemency
Until he granted him his life, and he
Was given to the queen, she to decide,
At her own will, whether he lived or died.
The queen then thanked the king with all her heart,
900   And one day, speaking to the knight apart
When the occasion seemed appropriate,
She said, "You are not out of danger yet,
For of your life you have no guarantee.
I'll grant you life if you can tell to me
905   What thing it is that women most desire.
Beware, and save your neck from iron most dire!
But if you cannot tell me right away,
I'll let you have a twelve-month and a day
To go and find an answer that may be,
910   For this great question, satisfactory.
Give me your word that you'll come back to face
My judgment, in good time, and in this place."

Woeful this knight was. But, well! now he knew
His former pleasures he must not pursue,
915   And so at last he chose to go away,
Pledged to return in twelve months and a day
With such an answer as God might provide.
He took his leave, and, riding far and wide,
He sought in every house and every place
920   Where he might find an answer, and the grace
To learn the thing that women love the most.
Wherever he went, though, ranging coast to coast,
He found upon this subject no one who
Agreed with others, no, not even two.
925   Some said that women love great riches best,

Some mentioned honor, some said jollyness,
Some said fine clothing, some said lust in bed,
And some said, often widowed, often wed.
Some said our hearts are most profoundly eased
930   When we've been nicely flattered and well-pleased,[11]
And that one's near the truth, it seems to me:
A man shall win us best with flattery.
Give us attention, some nice words, and lo!—
We're caught like birds in lime,[12] both high and low.
935   And some say that we women love the best
To do just as we please; as for the rest,
Not to have overbearing men despise
Our silliness, but tell us we are wise,
For truly there is none of us that live,
940   If we are hit where we are sensitive,
Who won't kick back then, even if it's true.
Just try it, and find out what we can do!
Because however bad we are within,
We want to be thought wise and free from sin.
945   And some say that we take delight if we
Are thought dependable and trustworthy,
And able to a single course to hold
And not reveal the things that we are told.
But that's a fantasy, not worth a penny.
950   Keep secrets? No, we women can't keep any.
Take Midas—would you like to hear the story?
Among the greater details of his glory
That Ovid tells, he had, so it appears,
Upon his head a pair of asses' ears.
955   These Midas kept, as well as he could do,
So subtly hidden from all others' view
That no one but his wife was in the know.
He loved her best, and trusted her also;
Therefore he begged her that to nobody
960   Would she reveal his foul deformity.
She swore that nothing, even should she win
The world for it, would tempt her to such sin

---

[11] Suddenly we hear the voice of the Wife of Bath, as she identifies with these women giving
their answers to the knight.

[12] This was a method for trapping birds for food. Lime was spread on a branch and the birds'
feet would stick to it.

As tell and so disgrace her husband's name;
Nor would she risk, by telling, her own shame.
965   But nonetheless, it seemed to her she died
With every thought of what she kept inside.
Around her heart, it seemed, it swelled and stirred
So violently, there must escape some word,
And since she dared to tell it to no man,
970   Down to a nearby marsh the lady ran.
Till she arrived, her heart was all on fire,
And like a bittern[13] booming in the mire,
Down to the water's edge her mouth she lay.
"Water," she said, "your sound must not betray
975   What I tell you alone where no one hears:
My husband has two great big ass's ears!
Now, then, my heart's at ease, for it is out.
I could not keep it in, beyond a doubt!"
And so, though for a while we may not peep,
980   As you can see, no secret can we keep.
It must get out. As for the story's end,
Read Ovid, and you'll find it there, my friend.[14]

This knight of whom my tale is specially,
When he saw that the answer might not be—
985   That is, what women love the most—so easy,
His spirits fell; his heart itself felt queasy.
But home he went, for he could not delay
The journey back; it almost was the day
He'd sworn to come. But when he chanced to ride
990   In all his woe, along the forest side,
He saw there in a circle twenty-four
Fair ladies dancing,[15] so he set his spur
And galloped toward the dance in hopes that he
Might learn the thing he sought so eagerly.

---

13   Bittern: an aquatic bird.

14   The story of Midas is in Book XI of Ovid's *Metamorphoses*. Chaucer has changed Ovid's tale to suit the teller (the Wife of Bath) and her story. It is worth reading the tale that Ovid tells not only for the conclusion, as Chaucer suggests, but to see who Ovid says knows about the ass's ears and cannot keep the secret; it is not Midas's wife. Such changes are typical of the way Chaucer manipulates a story to suit his purpose. Appropriation and manipulation of texts is also one of the Wife's most notable skills, as seen in her Prologue in *The Canterbury Tales*.

15   The dancing ladies reveal to an alert audience the nature of the hag that the knight sees immediately afterwards; see lines 860–61 above.

Part II: The Hag

995	But lo, indeed, before he got quite there,
	The dance had vanished, nor did he know where.
	No living creature anywhere was seen
	Except a woman sitting on the green.
	None uglier could be conceived, God knows.
1000	To meet the knight the ancient woman rose
	And said, "Sir knight, no road goes on[16] from here.
	Tell me what you are looking for, my dear.
	Perhaps, who knows, it will the better be.
	Old people know a lot of things," said she.
1005	"Old mother, dear," the knight said right away,
	"I am as good as dead unless I say
	What thing it is that women most desire.
	If you can tell me, well I'll pay your hire."
	"Pledge me your word," said she, "that you will do
1010	The very next thing that I require of you,
	If it lies in your power. Pledge by your hand.
	The answer you will have and my demand
	"Before night falls." "You have my word," said he.
	"Well then, indeed I dare to boast," said she,
1015	"That your life's safe, for I will stand by my
	Opinion, and your queen will say as I,
	And let's see if the proudest of them all,
	Wearing a noble headdress or high shawl,
	Would dare to contradict what I shall teach.
1020	Let us be gone now, without further speech."
	She whispered then a message in his ear
	And bade him to be glad and have no fear.
	When they arrived, the knight was heard to say
	That he had come as promised, on the day,
1025	And had the answer that would save his life.
	Then many a maiden, many a noble wife,
	And many a widow (they are very wise),
	And then the queen in judgment on a dais,
	Were all assembled, waiting there to hear,
1030	And then the knight was bidden to appear.

---

[16] No road goes on: i.e., he has come to a "dead end" in his quest.

Silence was called in order that he should
Before her Highness say, as best he could,
The thing that worldly women love the best.
The knight did not stand silent as a beast
1035   But gave them, in a manly voice and clear,
The answer so that all the court could hear.
"My liege lady, in general terms," said he,
"A woman most of all wants sovereignty.
A woman wants to have the power over
1040   Her husband just as much as any lover.
This is your greatest wish, though you may kill
Me for those words. I stand here at your will."
In all the court no woman, wife or maid
Or widow, contradicted what he said,
1045   And all agreed his life was well-deserved.

Up the old woman sprang, then, at that word,
She whom the knight upon the grass had seen.
"Mercy," she said, "my sovereign lady queen!"
"Before your court departs I want what's right.
1050   'Twas I who taught this answer to the knight,
For which he gave his word that he would do
The very first thing that I would ask him to,
Whatever it was, if in his power it lay.
Before this audience, sir knight, I pray,"
1055   Said she, "that you will take me for your wife,
For well you know that I have saved your life.
If I say false, deny it utterly!"

Part III: Keeping Trouthe

The knight replied, "Alas, and woe is me!
Too well I know that promise I did make,
1060   But choose another thing, please, for God's sake!
Take all I have, but let my body go!"
"A curse on both of us if I did so,"
She cried, "for though I'm ugly, old, and poor,
I wouldn't want all the metal or the ore
1065   That's buried underground or lies above
Unless I were your wife—also, your love!"
"My *love*?" said he. "No, my damnation. Oh,

That someone of my family[17] should know
Such a disgrace!" But this despondency
1070   Availed him nothing. It was clear that he
Was under obligation, so they wed.
He took his old wife then, and went to bed.

Some might find fault with me now, and aver
That I was negligent not to take care
1070   To tell you all the joy and celebration
There was at court, but as this accusation
I refute, my explanation shall
Be brief: there was no joy or feast at all,
But only heaviness of heart, for he
1080   Got married in the morning privately,
And all day afterwards hid like an owl,
Unhappy that his wife should look so foul.

Great was the woe the knight had in his thought
When to their wedding bed the two were brought.
1085   He twisted and he turned there in the bed,
Until his wife, who lay there smiling, said,
"Bless you, my dear husband, is it true
That every married knight behaves like you?
Is this the custom of King Arthur's bold
1090   And noble court, that every knight be cold?
I am your own beloved and your wife.
I am the woman who has saved your life—
And certainly not wronged you. Is it right
That you behave like this on our first night?
1095   You act like someone who has lost his wits.
What is my guilt? For God's sake tell me! It's
Possible I shall fix it, if I can."
"Fix it!" cried he. "Alas, just understand,
No one can ever fix it, for it's *you*!
1100   You are so old, and you're so ugly too,
And furthermore, you're of a class so low,
It's little wonder that I'm tossing so.
I wish my heart would split right in my chest!"

---

[17] My family: he is saying that it is a disgrace for someone of a rank so high as his to have to marry someone like this old woman found by the wayside. He sees her as his "damnation" socially, for he has not yet acquired any moral values.

1105

"Is this," she said, "the cause of your unrest?"
"It certainly is," he said, "and no surprise."
"Now, sir," she said, "all this I could revise
If I decided to, in two or three
Short days, if you would be polite to me.[18]

The Sermon

1110

1115

1120

1125

1130

"But speaking of nobility, that which is
Descended out of ancient wealth and riches,
To say that this can make you 'noble' men,
That's arrogance, and isn't worth a hen.
Look for the virtuous person; look for who
In private as in public tries to do,
Always, whatever noble deeds he can—
That's who is the greatest nobleman.
We claim from Christ our old nobility,
Not from our ancestors' heredity,
For though they give us all their heritage
Whereby we claim a noble lineage,
Yet they cannot bequeath the virtuous
Way they lived, or transfer onto us
What people praised as their nobility,
And bid us follow them in that degree.
Well did that wise, poetic Florentine
Called Dante say exactly what I mean.
Look, I am rhyming Dante's tale like him:
'Rare is the tree that lifts to every limb
The sap of merit, for God wills it should be
From Him that we claim our nobility.'[19]
For from our elders nothing may we claim
But temporal things that men may hurt or maim.
And everybody knows (it's plain to see),
If nobleness were planted naturally

---

[18] This assertion by the hag of her power to change reveals her identity as a fairy, probably the fairy queen herself (see lines 860–61 above). The "sermon" that follows, by which she educates the knight, corresponds to the brief admonition to Amans by Genius at the end of Gower's tale; it addresses a number of issues either emphasized or implied by the story. There is nothing like it in any other version of the Loathly Lady tale.

[19] Lines 1128 through the first half of 1129 are quoted directly from John Ciardi's translation of Dante's *Purgatory* 7: 121–22 (New York: New American Library, 1957), 87. The rest is paraphrased.

1135   Within a certain lineage, down the line
       In public and in private one would find
       Them doing all the duties of the noble.
       To harbor vice then they would not be able.

       "Put fire inside the darkest house between
1140   Here and the Caucasus Mountains, then
       Have people shut the doors and go away:
       The fire will still burn on, as bright and gay
       As if some twenty men beheld it there
       Performing its natural duty—this I swear
1145   Upon my life—till it dies naturally.
       You see by this how your nobility
       Is not annexed to long-descended wealth,
       Because not everyone behaves himself
       As does the fire, according to its kind.
1150   God knows that men may very often find
       A lord's son doing things of little worth,
       While wanting to be praised for noble birth
       And being born into a noble house
       Where many ancestors were virtuous.
1155   But if he does not want to follow on
       The way of those good ancestors now gone,
       He is not noble, be he duke or earl,
       For low and sinful deeds create a churl.
       All you call 'gentilesse'[20] is but fame
1160   Of forebears, for the goodness of their name.
       It's something separate from you, for your own
       Nobility must come from God alone.
       Thence comes our 'gentilesse,' from His grace,
       And it is not bequeathed us with our place.
1165   Think how, as one who reads Valerius knows,
       The king named Tullius Hostillius[21] rose
       From poverty to high-ranked nobleness.

---

[20] *Gentilesse* (four syllables: gen-til-ess-ah) is an important word in Chaucer's vocabulary. It shares the ambiguity of "nobility," the word used to translate *gentilesse* in this tale, for in addition to referring to rank, it includes nuances of ethical and courtly behavior, and even simple politeness. The word recurs at important points in other Chaucer tales as well. In the sermon that he has the Wife of Bath place in the mouth of her story's hag, Chaucer is pointing out the word's ambiguity and defining its ethical meaning.

[21] Tullius Hostillius: a mythical Roman king.

Seneca and Boethius[22] both express
Also, what anyone may see who reads,
1170   That nobleness must come from noble deeds.
And therefore, my dear husband, I conclude:
That though my ancestors were poor and rude,[23]
I still dare hope that God on high may give
Me grace to live in virtue while I live.
1175   I shall be noble, then, when I begin
To live in virtue and abandon sin.

"As for reproving me for being poor,
God, whom we all believe in, opted for
Poverty as a chosen way of life,
1180   And surely, every man or maid or wife
Can understand that Jesus, Heaven's king,
Would never choose to do a lowly thing.
Elective poverty is an honest way
To live, as Seneca and others say.
1185   A person satisfied with poverty,
Even without a shirt, lives wealthily.
He who covets is the poorer man,
Desiring property he never can
Possess. But he with naught who nothing craves
1190   Is rich, though you may class him with the knaves.[24]
True poverty, they say, sings properly.
As Juvenal says of it, 'How merrily
The poor man when he walks along the way
Before a gang of thieves may sing and play!'
1195   Poverty, though a virtue all despise,
Makes people work the harder, I surmise,
Improving, too, the wisdom of the man
Who takes it with such patience as he can.
Poverty has this virtue: though it seems
1200   Miserable, it is something no one dreams
Of challenging. Indeed, when one is low,
It's poverty that will make one want to know
Both God and self. It magnifies, for through
Its lens a man sees whether friends are true.

---

[22] Seneca and Boethius: late Roman philosophers.
[23] Rude: uneducated.
[24] Knaves: peasants, not wicked people.

1205 Therefore, sir, since I don't harm your life,
Reprove no more for poverty your wife.

"Now, sir, for age you've reprimanded me,
And though, indeed, there's no authority
For this in books, yet gentlemen will hold
1210 It proper to be courteous to the old,
Calling an old man 'father,' and I guess a
Book exists about such 'gentilesse.'
'Ugly and old' you've called me to my face.
You need not be in terror, in that case,
1215 Of cuckoldry,[25] because my ugliness
Will be a guarantee of faithfulness.

Conclusion

"But since I know what causes you delight,
I'll satisfy your worldly appetite.
So choose now only one of these," she said:
1220 "To have me old and ugly till I'm dead,
And be to you a true and humble wife,
And never to displease you all my life,
Or else to have me young and fair, and take
Your chances on this choice, how it may make
1225 Your house become well-known because of me—
And other places too, it might well be.
Now you decide which way you want your bride."
The knight thought deeply, ponderously he sighed,
And at the last he said as you may hear:
1230 "My lady and my love, and wife so dear,
I put myself in your wise governance.
Choose for yourself which one will most enhance
Our pleasure, and respect for me and you.
It matters not to me which of the two
1235 You choose, for pleasing you now pleases me."
"Then have I got the upper hand," said she,
"Since I may choose and govern as I say?"
"Yes," said the knight, "I think it's best that way."
"Kiss me," she said. "And now, upon my troth,

---

[25] Of cuckoldry: being a victim of adultery.

1240 Let us not quarrel, for I shall be both,
   Pretty and also good, that is to say,
   And may I die a madwoman, I pray,
   If I'm not also just as good and true
   As ever wife was since the world was new.
1245 If I am not as lovely to be seen
   As any lady, empress, maid, or queen
   Upon this earth, from east to farthest west,
   Do with my life and death as you think best.
   Now cast the curtain up, my dear, and see!"

1250 And when the knight had seen how changed was she,
   That she was young and also very fair,
   He caught her in his arms right then and there.
   He felt his heart bathed in a bath of bliss.
   A thousand times he bent again to kiss
1255 His wife, who chose to "honor and obey"
   And make his life a joy in every way.
   And thus in joy they lived until the end
   Of both their lives, and may the good Lord send
   Husbands all meek and young and good in bed,
1260 And vigor to outlive the men we wed,
   And may Jesú[26] abbreviate the lives
   Of those who won't be governed by their wives.
   As for men old and angry, tight with pence,[27]
   A plague upon them for their truculence![28]

---

[26] Spelled Jhesu in the original (Jesus).

[27] Pence is the British plural of penny.

[28] The Wife's change of tone here snatches us out of the fairy world as suddenly as the remarks of Genius snatch us out of "The Tale of Florent," but she is so alive that we can imaginatively grasp the emotional cause of her outburst: on awakening from her own storytelling, she realizes, to her dismay, that "living happily ever after" occurs only in a fairy tale. Readers are often distressed by this happy ending also, many feeling that the rapist offender has not been adequately punished. The standard reply that this story is about rehabilitation rather than punishment does not really absolve Chaucer of his failure to tie up some loose ends in regard to that crime. On the other hand, he does rescue the Loathly Lady from her role as fairy-tale victim and reconceive her as a figure of wisdom and power.

CHAPTER 3

Thomas of Erceldoune

"Thomas of Erceldoune," a romance of the Scottish Borders, has fallen between the cracks of genre. That may be why it has been relatively ignored by scholars; neither Severs in his overview of Middle English romance[1] nor Rice in her bibliography[2] even mentions it. It lies somewhere between romance, versified prophecy (a medieval genre of its own), and later ballad. More precisely, it is composed of these first two genres, romance and prophecy patched together, and put into quasi-ballad form, the third genre. J.A.H. Murray, who later became general editor of

---

[1] J. Burke Severs, *A Manual of the Writings in Middle English, 1050–1500, I. Romances* (New Haven: Connecticut Academy of Arts and Sciences, 1967).

[2] Joanne A. Rice, *Middle English Romance: An Annotated Bibliography, 1955–1985* (New York: Garland, 1987).

the *Oxford English Dictionary* (*OED*), published the only serious edition of this work in 1875.[3]

Thomas of Erceldoune, the protagonist of the tale, was a real person who lived in the late thirteenth century in the town in the Scottish Borders from which he gets his name, a town now called Earldon. Huntly Banks is a real place nearby, and even the Eildon Tree, an important site in the poem, had an actual existence, its former location being marked now by a stone in the Eildon Hills about half a mile east of Huntly Banks.[4] Thomas is referred to several times outside of this romance in both legal and fictional contexts,[5] and prophecies purporting to be spoken by him began to be recorded not long after his death.[6] The earliest of the five manuscripts of his romance, providing an exciting narrative explanation for Thomas's gift, is dated 1440; and in early modern times several ballad versions of the narrative part of the romance emerged (Child ballad 37, "Thomas Rymer").[7] Sir Walter Scott's probably composite and certainly "improved" ballad of "True Thomas" in his 1802 *Minstrelsy of the Scottish Border* is the most coherent version of the story after the romance, presenting Thomas the story-teller as less than pleased by his fairy "gift" of a tongue that must always speak true.[8] Scott's ballad is offered as an appendix following the romance below.

---

[3] J.A.H. Murray, ed., *The Romance and Prophecies of Thomas of Erceldoune*, EETS 61 (London: N. Trübner, 1875). Murray's text is now available online at <http://www.tam-lin.org/texts/thomas.html#R>.

   Curiously, TEAMS (The Consortium for the Teaching of the Middle Ages) offers an edition of "Thomas of Erceldoune's Prophecy" from MS Harley 2253, c. 1330, while neglecting the later narrative of how Thomas acquired his prophetic gift.

[4] Murray l–lii.

[5] For example, "Blind Hary" in his life in verse "The Wallace" has Thomas active around 1296; at lines 2: 288–350 of this poem Thomas makes a cameo appearance and has a conversation with a priest in which he says that Wallace will three times oust the English from Scotland (2: 346–50). See *The Wallace: Selections*, edited by Anne McKim, available at <http://www.lib.rochester.edu/camelot/teams/wallint.htm> (originally published in *The Wallace: Selections* [Kalamazoo, MI: Medieval Institute Publications, 2003]). For more about the historical and literary background of the story, see Lizanne Henderson and Edward J. Cowan, *Scottish Fairy Belief: A History* (East Linton, Scotland: Tuckwell Press, 2001), 147–51 and notes. (I am grateful to Stella Longland for directing me to this book.) The following online source (popular, with blog) contains more about Thomas, with links: <http://bestoflegends.org/ballads/thomas.html>.

[6] Henderson and Cowan offer evidence suggesting that "True Thomas enjoyed a reputation for prophecy in his own lifetime" (147).

[7] Francis James Child, *The English and Scottish Popular Ballads*, vol. I (New York: Dover, 1965 [first pub. 1882–84]), 317–29.

[8] One tradition identifies Thomas as a borderlands horse dealer (Henderson and Cowan 151), a profession in which complete honesty was not expected and might be thought detrimental to trade. Scott's ballad is reproduced by Child in *Popular Ballads*, vol. I, 325–26.

The source of the fairy abduction story in "Thomas of Erceldoune" is peculiar and fascinating. Apparently the writer of the romance, looking around for a suitable story to attach to this Scottish prophet whose fame in his homeland by then rivaled Merlin's, found one that he could appropriate in a French story about Ogier le Danois. Originally Ogier was imagined as one of the twelve peers of France who aided Charlemagne during the time the Moors were threatening Europe,[9] but famous heroes have to come from somewhere, and if they evoke sufficient popular interest, a back story will appear. According to his back story, Ogier, or Holger the Dane (originally not Danish at all), was abducted by Morgan le Fay ("the Fairy") and kept by her in Avalon until his presence was required to fight for France. After Ogier rescues France from the foes of Christendom, he returns with Morgan to her otherworld country. The particular episode that links this story clearly to that of Thomas is Ogier's misidentification of Morgan when he first sees her approach him in her glamorous fairy attire. He thinks she is the Virgin Mary and addresses her accordingly; she replies that she has never aspired to such high rank and then identifies herself as the fairy she is.[10] The ballad-like narrative of "Thomas of Erceldoune" also bears a relationship of some kind to the genuine ballad titled "Tam Lin," included in Appendix A of this book. Both stories concern fairy abductions and portray interesting gender relationships and conflicts, yet, despite their engaging plots, both are neglected in discussions of romance, presumably because they are so late and marginal to the genre.[11]

Those familiar with Chaucer's "Wife of Bath's Tale" will find especially intriguing the way "Thomas of Erceldoune" associates the Loathly Lady theme with rape and agency in lines 64–101. Here it seems as though

---

9   The famous story of this conflict, greatly fictionalized, is the French *Song of Roland* (c. 1100), in which Ogier first appears. He is also the hero of his own *chanson de geste*, *La Chevalerie d'Ogier de Danemarche*, explored in some detail by Willem P. Gerritsen and Anthony G. van Melle in their *Dictionary of Medieval Heroes* (Woodbridge, Suffolk: Boydell Press, 1998), 186–88, and he is the hero of further stories in French, Italian, Catalan, and Icelandic (Gerritsen and Melle 188). He is identified as one of the twelve peers of France and named several times in "The Sultan of Babylon," an early fifteenth-century Middle English romance (available online at <http://www.lib.rochester.edu/camelot/teams/sultfrm.htm>). "Holger," in his modern aspect definitely a Dane, continues to be popular; see Gerritsen and Melle for details. The basic story is excitingly retold by A.R. Hope-Moncrieff in *The Romance of Chivalry* (North Hollywood, CA: Newcastle Publishing, 1976), 249–76.

10   Francis J. Child, who tells in detail the Ogier back story (based on a French version of Ogier's *enfances*), refers in a footnote to a French book, now lost, containing "The Visions of Ogier in Fairy Land." Quoting a passage from that book reprinted elsewhere, he suggests that this French story might have made the relationship between Thomas Rhymer and Ogier clearer (I: 319).

11   Henderson and Cowan's book is an exception (see n.5 above).

the fairy is genuinely powerless to fend off Thomas, and his abuse of her turns her "loathly." (One could contemplate the psychology of Thomas's revised view of the lady once he has raped her.) Afterwards, when one might justly expect her to punish Thomas, instead she whisks him off to fairyland, where her beauty, to his astonishment, is renewed. The casual rape followed by fairy reward is much more disturbing in this story than in Chaucer's tale, where the offending knight appears at least to have learned a lesson, kindly but firmly taught. Chaucer's story is concerned with chivalrous behavior, however, whereas "Thomas of Erceldoune" has other concerns: at the beginning of Fytt II[12] the fairy offers Thomas his choice of skill in music or words, "to harp or carp," and when he chooses "carping" (clever talk) she gives him the ability to tell it true, i.e., the power of prophecy. The back story has been constructed specifically to arrive at this point, and, despite references to Heaven and Hell, the author is not much interested in moral issues.

All of Fytt I is offered here, but only the first few stanzas of Fytt II, containing the fairy's gift. In this modernization I have broken the continuous text of the original romance into its obvious abab-rhymed stanzas. A curious feature of Fytt I is the way it begins with a first-person narrator, modulates with the lady's description into third-person narrative, and then near the end slips briefly back to the narrator speaking as if he himself were Thomas (line 209). The May morning scene with which the romance opens is a cliché that happens to be very pretty and is thus an appropriate point of entry for the beautiful fairy lady.

---

[12]   The word "fytt" is a medieval term for a section of a work, usually of a long poem.

Thomas of Erceldoune

Fytt I

As I walked out alone one day,
My mind fixed fast on my lament,
Upon a merry morning of May
Along by Huntly Banks I went.

5　　The throstle and the jay I heard,
　　The thrush lamenting as she sang,
　　And bell-like sang the wodwal bird[13]
　　So all the woods around me rang.

　　Alone in longing as I lay
10　　Underneath a seemly tree,
　　I saw afar a lady gay
　　Come riding over a lovely lea.[14]

　　If I should sit until doomsday
　　And work my tongue continually,
15　　The beauty of that lady gay
　　Could never be described by me.

　　Her palfrey[15] was a dapple-gray.
　　Never have I seen such a one!
　　The lady, fair as a summer's day,
20　　Was shining brightly as the sun.

　　Her saddle was of ivory bone
　　And was a seemly sight to see,
　　Set with many a precious stone
　　And studded about with crapotée.[16]

25　　Plentiful gems of the Orient glowed.
　　Her hair was hanging loose and long.

---

[13] Wodwal bird: oriole.

[14] Lea: meadow.

[15] Palfrey: riding horse as opposed to warhorse.

[16] Crapotée: possibly quartz.

All over that lovely lea she rode
And whistled a while, then sang a song.

Her girths of noble silk they were,
30   The buckles all of beryl made.
Her stirrups were of the crystal clear,
And all with pearl was overlaid.

Of purple gems her payetrelle,[17]
The crupper[18] gold with embroidery.
35   Her bridle shone like the golden bells
That hung on each side, three and three.

Three greyhounds on a leash she led,
Running beside her seven more.
A hunting horn on her neck she had
40   And arrows tucked in the belt she wore.

Thomas lay and beheld that sight
From underneath a seemly tree.
He said, "Yon's Mary, most of might,
Who bore the Child that died for me!

45   "Unless I speak with that lady bright,
My heart will surely break in three![19]
Now I shall run with all my might
To meet her at the Eildon Tree."

So quickly, Thomas, up he rose
50   And ran across both hill and lea,
And if it be as the story goes,
He met her at the Eildon Tree.

And kneeling down upon his knee,
He said, beneath that greenwood spray,
55   "Lovely lady, rue on me,
Queen of Heaven, as you well may!"

---

[17] Payetrelle: breast-armor of a horse.

[18] Crupper: a strap going under the horse's tail to hold the saddle in place.

[19] Break in three: standard for broken hearts in romance (for the rhyme).

Then spoke that lady mild of thought,
"Thomas, let such notions be.
The Queen of Heaven I am not,
60   Nor ever took such high degree.

"I am of another country, though,
And after the wildwood deer I ride.
That's why I am appareled so,
My greyhounds running at my side."

65   "If you, appareled with such show,
Come in your folly riding by,
For love, lady, as you must know,
You give me leave with you to lie!"

She said, "That would a folly be.
70   Thomas, let me go I pray.
That sin, I tell you certainly,
All my beauty will take away.

"Now, lovely lady, rue on me,
And evermore with thee I'll dwell.
75   Here my troth I pledge to thee,
Whether you go to Heaven or Hell."

"Earthly man, you'll do me harm,
And yet you shall have all your joy.
Believe it well, you've chosen wrong,
80   For all my beauty you will destroy."

And then dismounted the lady fair
Underneath that greenwood spray,
And as the story tells it, there
He seven times beside her lay.

85   She said, "It pleases you to play.[20]
What maid in bower may deal with thee?
You've done me harm this livelong day.
I pray you, Thomas, let me be."

---

[20] Play: have sex.

Up in that place then Thomas stood,
90   And he beheld that lady gay.
Her hair hung tangled from her head.
Her eyes seemed out that were so gray.[21]

Now gone was all her rich array,
And she was clothed in rags instead.
95   One leg was black, the other gray,
And all her body was gray as lead.

Underneath the greenwood spray
Thomas looked upon that sight.
"Alas," he said, "alas, this place!
100   In faith this is a doleful plight.
How you have faded in your face
Who like the sun were shining bright!"

"Thomas, take leave of sun and moon
And all the life that grows on tree.
105   This twelve-month with me you'll be gone
And middle earth you shall not see."

He knelt then down upon his knee
And prayed, beneath the greenwood spray,
"Lovely lady, rue on me,
110   Queen of Heaven, as you best may."[22]

"Alas," he said, "alas for me.
I think my deeds will cause me woe.
Jesus, my soul I commit to thee,
Wherever my body's bones may go."

115   She led him in at Eildon hill
Underneath a secret lea,
Where black as midnight the waters chill
Rose up higher than his knee.

---

[21] Gray: i.e., blue.

[22] Here Thomas prays to the "real" Queen of Heaven, the Virgin Mary, but the context makes the intended recipient of his prayer curiously ambiguous.

And when it seemed three days had passed,
120   And he heard only the river sigh,
"Oh, woe is me," he said at last,
"For lack of food I'll surely die!"

She led him into a garden fair
Where fruit was growing beyond the gate.
125   Ready and ripe were apple and pear
And also the damson-plum and date.

And there were also berry and fig,
And nightingales that built a nest,
And parrots flying from twig to twig,
130   And thrushes singing that took no rest.

He hurried to pluck like a person who
Was faint with hunger, and food has seen.
But she said, "Leave them, Thomas, or you
Shall soon be taken by the fiend.

135   "For if you pluck, it's true to say,
Your soul will go to the fire of Hell
And come out never until doomsday,
But always there in torment dwell.

"Come lay your head down on my knee,
140   Thomas, truly I command.
The fairest sight then you shall see
That ever saw anyone of your land."

He quickly did then what she bade
And laid his head upon her knee.
145   To please her now he was so glad,
And then once more to him said she:

"Yonder fair highway can you see,
Where over the mountain high it leads?
That goes to Heaven where souls may be
150   Who've passed the pain of their misdeeds.

"Now can you see that second way
Where through the underbrush it lies?
That road goes on, they truly say,
All the way to Paradise.

155   "Can you see yet a third way go
Down along yon grassy plain?
That way some souls, with grief and woe,
Will go to suffer endless pain.

"Now can you see the fourth way pass
160   Yonder, deep into the dell?
Yonder road is the way, alas,
Into the burning fires of Hell.

"And see you yonder castle fair
Standing upon the hill so high?
165   There's nothing to match it anywhere,
Of town or tower, beneath the sky.

"Forsooth, Thomas, it is my own,
Shared with the king. But Thomas, stay!
I would rather be hanged and drawn
170   Than let him know that with me you lay!

"So when we come to that castle fair,
I pray that courteous you will be,
And whatsoever they ask you there,
Be sure you speak to none but me.

175   "My lord eats meals there every day
Served by thirty knights fair and free.
I'll sit upon the dais and say
I took your speech[23] beyond the sea."

Thomas stood there still as stone
180   And looked upon that lady gay.
She now as fair and lovely shone
As long before on her palfrey gray.

---

[23]   I took your speech: i.e., she claims she will pretend to have enchanted him to make him dumb (silent)..

And now her hounds were leashed again
And sated with the blood of deer.
185   She blew her horn with might and main
As to the castle they drew near.

She went in at the castle door
Followed by Thomas upon her heel.
Fair maidens came there then, before
190   The lady courteously to kneel.

Harp and fiddle they carried in
And also gittern and psaltry gay.
They entered with lute and mandolin,
And all kinds of music did they play.

195   But the greatest marvel, Thomas thought,
As he stood there upon the floor,
Was how some fifty stags were brought
By porters in at the castle door.[24]

The hounds were lapping up their blood
200   As cooks with the knives of butchers came
To carve the venison into food.
They slashed away as in some mad game.

The knights were dancing, three and three,
And there was revelry and play,
205   As noble ladies, fair and free,
Sat and sang in their clothing gay.

Thomas dwelt in that pleasant place
And utterly content was he,
Until one day (may I have grace)
210   My lovely lady said to me:

"Get ready, Thomas, to go again,
For longer here you may not be.
Hurry with all your might and main.
I'll take you back to the Eildon Tree."

---

[24] Perhaps Thomas is amazed because he thinks he has been with the lady all the time, so he wonders when her great hunt could have taken place. Time plays tricks in the otherworld.

215 Thomas replied with heavy face,
     "Lovely lady, let me be,
     For surely, lady, in this place
     I have not been more days than three!"

     "Forsooth, then, Thomas, I have to say
220 That you've been here three years and more.
     But longer here you may not stay,
     And now I will explain wherefore.

     "Tomorrow the fiend comes out of Hell
     Among this folk to fetch his sheep.
225 Since you're so big and handsome as well,
     I know you're one he'll wish to keep.

     "For all the gold there may ever be
     From now until the end of time,
     You never shall be betrayed by me,
230 Therefore I advise you to go home."

     She brought him back to the Eildon Tree,
     Underneath that greenwood spray,
     On Huntly Bank where it's good to be
     And birds are singing night and day.

235 She said, "On yonder mountain gray,
     Thomas, my falcon builds a nest.
     Upon a falcon the earl will prey,
     So there is nowhere it may rest.[25]

     "Farewell, Thomas, I'm going away
240 Over the grasses sere and brown."
     Look, the fit's over! But one could say
     More about Thomas of Erceldoune.

---

[25] This falcon metaphor is not in the oldest manuscript (Thornton), so it may be a later addition. Mysterious as it is, the falcon is a standard metaphor for a lover in courtly poetry. In his famous sonnet "The Windhover," Gerard Manley Hopkins adapts this metaphor representing the knight-lover to represent Christ. On the other hand, in this area settled by Celts and Vikings, since the goddess-shaman was familiar in both cultures, the falcon could represent the fairy's own bird-soul or her bird form. The Norse goddess Freyja's falcon cloak that gives the wearer the power of flight is mentioned near the beginning of the Eddic poem *Thrymskvida*, for example, and the Irish Morrigan is also able to assume bird form, as a raven.

Fytt II

"Farewell, Thomas, I'm going away.
I may no longer remain with thee."
"Give me a token, lady gay,
That I may say I spoke with thee."

5   "To harp or carp, wherever you go,
Thomas, I'm giving a choice to thee."
"Though harping is good," he said, "I know
Tongue is chief of minstrelsy."

"Then any tale you want to tell,
10   Thomas, you'll never a liar be.
Wherever you go, by forest or dell,
I pray you speak no ill of me.

"Farewell, Thomas, I'm going away.
I may no longer remain with thee."
15   "But wait, my lovely lady, stay
And tell some wondrous thing to me."

"Thomas, hear what I say to thee," etc.

[Here the prophecies begin.]

Appendix: The Ballad of Thomas Rymer

Thi his ballad, number 37-C in Francis J. Child's collection, *The English and Scottish Popular Ballads*, first appeared in print in volume II of Sir Walter Scott's *Minstrelsy of the Scottish Border* (1802). In general the ballad clearly derives from the romance "Thomas of Erceldoune." Folklorists frown on the way Scott liked to "improve" the ballads he learned from traditional singers or from manuscripts of their songs, but in my opinion this version with elements from two variants (Child's numbers 37-A and 37-B) works very well. Despite the sobriquet "true Thomas" at the beginning, Thomas's prophetic powers are not mentioned in the ballad. On the contrary, when in stanza 17 the fairy gives him "the tongue that can never lie," Thomas is sarcastic about the value of a gift that will profit him neither in commerce (at the fair) nor courtship (tryst).

The Scots dialect is not so difficult to read once one realizes that the final sounds of words are often omitted (*wi'* for *with*, *o* for *of*, etc.), as are medial consonants (*siller* for *silver*, *taen* for *taken*); that 'i' and 'y' are interchangeable (*fyne* for *fine*); and that 'o' often becomes 'a' (*belong* becomes *belang*, *rode* becomes *rade*). Other words of which the meaning is not obvious are glossed in footnotes,[26] and stanzas rather than lines are numbered. No liberties have been taken with the text.

---

[26] The online *Dictionary of the Scots Language* at <http://www.dsl.ac.uk/dsl/index.html> has been useful for this task.

1   TRUE Thomas lay on Huntlie bank,
     A ferlie[27] he spied wi his ee,
    And there he saw a lady bright,
     Come riding down by the Eildon Tree.

2   Her shirt was o the grass-green silk,
     Her mantle o the velvet fyne,
    At ilka tett[28] o her horse's mane
     Hang fifty siller bells and nine.

3   True Thomas, he pulld aff his cap,
     And louted[29] low down to his knee:
    "All hail, thou mighty Queen of Heaven!
     For thy peer on earth I never did see."

4   "O no, O no, Thomas," she said,
     "That name does not belang to me.
    I am but the queen of fair Elfland,
     That am hither come to visit thee.

5   "Harp and carp,[30] Thomas," she said,
     "Harp and carp along wi me,
    And if ye dare to kiss my lips,
     Sure of your bodie I will be."

6   "Betide me weal,[31] betide me woe,
     That weird shall never daunton me."[32]
    Syne[33] he has kissed her rosy lips,
     All underneath the Eildon Tree.

---

[27] Ferlie: wonder.

[28] Ilka tett: each strand.

[29] Louted: bowed.

[30] Carp: talk, converse.

[31] Betide me weal: befall me well, etc., i.e., whether good or ill befalls me.

[32] Weird ... daunton me: fate ... daunt me.

[33] Syne: then.

7   "Now, ye maun[34] go wi me," she said,
       "True Thomas, ye maun go wi me,
     And ye maun serve me seven years,
       Thro weal or woe, as may chance to be."

8   She mounted on her milk-white steed,
       She's taen True Thomas up behind,
     And aye wheneer her bridle rung,
       The steed flew swifter than the wind.

9   O they rade on, and farther on—
       The steed gaed swifter than the wind—
     Untill they reached a desart wide,
       And living land was left behind.

10   "Light down, light down, now, True Thomas,
       And lean your head upon my knee.
     Abide and rest a little space,
       And I will shew you ferlies three.

11   "O see ye not yon narrow road,
       So thick beset with thorns and briers?
     That is the path of righteousness,
       Tho after it but few enquires.

12   "And see not ye that braid braid road,
       That lies across that lily leven?[35]
     That is the path of wickedness,
       Tho some call it the road to heaven.

13   "And see not ye that bonny road,
       That winds about the fernie brae?[36]
     That is the road to fair Elfland,
       Where thou and I this night maun gae.[37]

---

[34] Maun: must.

[35] Leven: variant of lea, meadow.

[36] Brae: riverbank.

[37] Maun gae: must go.

14   "But, Thomas, ye maun hold your tongue,
        Whatever ye may hear or see,
    For, if you speak word in Elflyn land,
        Ye'll neer get back to your ain countrie."

15   O they rade on, and farther on,
        And they waded thro rivers aboon[38] the knee,
    And they saw neither sun nor moon,
        But they heard the roaring of the sea.

16   It was mirk mirk[39] night, and there was nae stern light,[40]
        And they waded thro red blude to the knee;
    For a' the blude that's shed on earth
        Rins[41] thro the springs o that countrie.

17   Syne they came on to a garden green,
        And she pu'd an apple frae a tree:
    "Take this for thy wages, True Thomas,
        It will give the tongue that can never lie."

18   "My tongue is mine ain," True Thomas said;
        "A gudely gift ye wad gie[42] to me!
    I neither dought[43] to buy nor sell,
        At fair or tryst where I may be.

19   "I dought neither speak to prince or peer,
        Nor ask of grace from fair ladye."
    "Now hold thy peace," the lady said,
        "For as I say, so must it be."

20   He has gotten a coat of the even[44] cloth,
        And a pair of shoes of velvet green,
    And till seven years were gane and past
        True Thomas on earth was never seen.

---

[38] Aboon: above.

[39] Mirk: dark.

[40] Nae stern light: no starlight.

[41] Rins: runs.

[42] Wad gie: would give.

[43] Dought: would be able.

[44] Even: perhaps this word should be "elven."

CHAPTER 4

Sir Orfeo

The story of the musician Orpheus seeking his dead wife Eurydice in the Underworld is one of the most retold stories in the Western world, because of both its intrinsic pathos and its metaphorical potential. It was told by the Greeks and Romans, and numerous times in English, beginning with King Alfred's translation of Boethius's *De conso-latione philosophiae* into Old English. It appears in modern times in forms as diverse as opera, the splendid film "Black Orpheus," and a young adult novel where the Orpheus character is a girl. Many of the great poets of our day have rewritten or alluded to the story, from Rainer Maria Rilke to Seamus Heaney. Denise Levertov's "A Tree Telling of Orpheus" is perhaps the most moving Orpheus poem since Virgil's, and deeply spiritual.[1]

The classical story is tragic: after his long quest, Orpheus almost saves his beloved wife. As a reward for his music, he has been told he may take her back to the upper world if he does not look back as she follows him

---

[1]   This poem from Levertov's book *Relearning the Alphabet* (New York: New Directions, 1970) may be read online at <http://www.poemhunter.com/poem/a-tree-telling-of-orpheus>.

there; but he loses her through an instant of inattention or lack of faith as he glances back to make sure she is coming. Translations of Ovid's tale in his *Metamorphoses* are readily available, including online, and a translation of Virgil's account from *The Georgics* is provided in an appendix to this romance. The late medieval Scottish poet Robert Henryson (fl. c. 1460–1500) imagines Orpheus's search for Eurydice as a lonely journey through the planetary spheres, where that great musician appropriately hears and appreciates their music. Later he finds, and loses, Eurydice:

> He blent [glanced] bakwart, and Pluto come anone,
> And unto hell agane with hir is gone.

When told as a romance, however, the story should be a tale of *gode likeing* ("excellent pleasure," 603) of which the melody is *swete* ("sweet," 606), and the English poet retells the tale as a Celtic story of the rescue of someone taken by the fairies, a plot with the happy ending suitable to romance. "Sir Orfeo" thus diverges from the classical story most significantly with the addition of elements from Celtic lore such as the beloved who is "taken" rather than dead and the fairy hunt,[2] and also the quasi-biblical parable of the loyal steward who looks after Orfeo's kingdom in his absence. Orfeo is not a king in the classical tale. Geraldine Barnes emphasizes how Orfeo employs stratagems (Middle English *gyn*) in two major scenes, first to win back his wife from the reluctant fairy king, and then to test the loyalty of his steward.[3] His cleverness is established right at the beginning of the romance when we are told that he was able to teach himself music because his wits were sharp (line 30).

The romance's "theme of love lost and found through the triumph of *gyn*" (Barnes 123) is certainly a major feature of "Sir Orfeo," and it is one of the Celtic features of the romance, since the folktale hero usually rescues the "taken" from fairies by wily manipulation. In folktales, however, the rescue involves outwitting someone in a way that leaves the evil abductor

---

[2]   See Dorena Allen's persuasive article, "Orpheus and Orfeo: The Dead and the *Taken*," *Medium Aevum* [MAE] 33 (1964): 102–11. According to Child, a ballad collected in the Shetland Islands before 1880 (Child ballad 19) derives from the "Sir Orfeo" version of the story (I 216). The plot is certainly similar, telling how a king retrieves his stolen queen from the fairies by playing his bagpipes so well that the fairy king offers him whatever he wants, but the same traditional Celtic story-type that influenced "Sir Orfeo," the rescue of someone who has been "taken" (abducted to the otherworld), could lie behind the ballad as well. In the Scottish tale of "The Stolen Bairn and the Sidh," it is a child that is taken by the Sidh (fairies) and his mother wins him back with her harp. The story is retold by Sorche Nic Leodhas in her Newbery Honor book *Thistle and Thyme, Tales and Legends from Scotland* (New York: Holt Rinehart and Winston, 1962), 46-61.

[3]   *Counsel and Strategy in Middle English Romance* (Cambridge: Brewer, 1993), 120–23.

angry and humiliated, whereas in this romance the mood is different: no one is left humiliated, and no one is, finally, represented as evil. Here, rather than putting either the fairy king or the steward in a bad light by outwitting them, Orfeo tests their *trawthe* (troth), or commitment to an ideal, and in each case finds it "true." This reading is more optimistic than that of Barnes, but such difference of interpretation is one of the delights offered by this tale; even in the costumery of romance, the story of Orpheus can be taken in many ways. One aspect of this Middle English version of the story about which everyone agrees is its high quality.

The prologue (as reconstructed by A.J. Bliss) identifies "Sir Orfeo" as a Breton lay, a brief and focused romance in rhyme associated with Brittany in France, and the opening lines (1–20) also provide an excellent, if broad, description of the contents of such a lay.[4]

---

[4] The present modernization mainly follows the Auchinleck manuscript in the edition by A.J. Bliss (Oxford: Oxford UP, 1954), with his reconstructed 38-line prologue (see the argument on pp. xlvi–iii of his edition). Four and a half lines from manuscript Ashmole 61 are inserted for clarity, as noted in the text. A great deal of help with interpretation and vocabulary was found in the edition by Anne Laskaya and Eve Salisbury, who follow Bliss closely, in *The Middle English Breton Lays*, published for the TEAMS Middle English Texts Series (Kalamazoo: Western Michigan University, 2001; also available from the "TEAMS Medieval Texts" site online at <http://www.lib.rochester.edu/camelot/teams/orfeo.htm>). Their introduction is especially recommended.

Sir Orfeo

Written we find and often read
(As clerics teach us at our need)
The rhyming lays a harper sings
Concerning many wondrous things,
5   Some of war and some of woe,
And some of joy and mirth also,
And some of guile and treacherous men
Or things occurring but now and then,
And some are ribald or a joke,
10   And many are of fairy folk.
Of all things, though, we might think of,
What they most concern is love.
In Brittany these lays were wrought,
Invented there and hither brought,
15   Adventures transformed into lays
Of things befalling in former days.
The Bretons, when their kings would hear
Of any marvel, far or near,
Took up their harps and, like a game,
20   Composed a lay, gave it a name.
Of these adventures that befell,
I can tell some, but not all.
So hark, my lords, if you would know
The story of Sir Orfeo.

25   Orfeo, more than anything,
Liked to take up his harp and sing.
The most professional harper would
Praise him, his harping was so good.
He taught himself to play the harp,
30   Applying his wits (yes, they were sharp)
So well that there was not, I swear,
A better harper anywhere.
If Orfeo sat down and gave
A concert, no one, prince or knave—
35   No one in all the world—could hear
And not imagine he was near

All the joys of Paradise,
Such music in his harping was!

And he was also a king, I've heard,
40 In England a respected lord,
A stalwart man and hardy, who
Was generous and courtly, too.
His father's line from Pluto came,
His mother's shared King Juno's fame;
45 Each was formerly thought to be,
For valor, a divinity.[5]
This king would often stay in Thrace,
A well-defended, noble place
(For Winchester was thought, back then,
50 The same as Thrace by learned men).
He had a lovely queen, and this
Good lady's name was Herodis,
The fairest lady of that day
Who walked in flesh and bone, they say—
55 And full of love and tenderness.
No tongue her beauty can express.

It so befell in early May,
When skies were bright and warm all day,
And past were all the winter showers,
60 And every field was full of flowers,
And blossoms bloomed on every tree,
With everything growing happily,
That Herodis went out that day
With two of her sweet maids, to play.[6]
65 In early morning they went out
And in an orchard walked about
To see the flowers blossoming
And hear the birds of springtime sing.

---

5 The attribution of descent from the gods was a medieval custom—but of course Juno was a goddess. Moreover, as a Christian poet, this writer follows Christian tradition in euhemerizing the gods (denying their divinity), while accepting them as powerful, heroic beings. Simply by naming Pluto and Juno, the poet places the story of Orfeo in "antiquity," and then in an aside at lines 49–50 he appropriates the ancient story for his English audience by relocating Grecian Thrace at the town of Winchester in southern England.

6 Play: enjoy themselves.

They sat down there, the ladies three,
70   Underneath an impe-tree,[7]
And fairly soon the lovely queen
Fell sound asleep upon the green.
The maidens did not dare to wake
Their lady, but let her lie and take
75   Her rest, until the sun had crept
Past noon. And still the lady slept.
But then she woke up suddenly
And cried out very miserably.
She wrung her hands and kicked her feet,
80   And scratched her cheeks that were so sweet,
And ripped apart her velvet dress,
And went quite crazy with distress.
The maidens with her did not dare
To linger longer, so the pair
85   Left their lady and hurried home
To tell both squire and knight to come
Because their queen was going mad
And must be held, it was so bad.
Knights and ladies began to run,
90   And sixty damosels, everyone,
And in the orchard they found the queen
And took her up from the grass so green,
And brought her to her bed, and then
Very securely tucked her in.
95   But she wept constantly for woe,
Desiring to get up and go.

When he received this news, the king
Was sorrier than anything.
With ten knights Orfeo came to see
100   His queen, came through the door, and he
Looked down and said with pity strong:
"My dearest love, what can be wrong?
You've always been so calm and quiet,
And now you are creating riot.
105   Your body was so fair, before
Your fingernails ripped and tore.

---

7   Impe: grafted. This term is so important in the story that it seems appropriate to retain the Middle English word.

Alas, your rosy cheeks are wan
Like those of someone dead and gone.
Your lovely fingers, long and slim,
110   Are bloody and pale, their brightness dim.
Alas, at me your lovely eyes
Now gaze as at one you despise.
My lady dear, your mercy I
Beseech you, darling, do not cry.
115   Just tell me what went wrong, and how,
And what I can do to fix it now."
She then grew calmer finally,
And weeping hard but quietly,
Replied to his kind inquiry so:
120   "Alas, my dear love Orfeo,
Since first we were together, we
Have never spoken angrily.
Always I have loved just you,
As my own life. You've loved me too.
125   But we will have to part today.
Whatever you do, I cannot stay."
"Alas, I am forlorn!" said he.
"Where will you go? Who will you see?
Wherever you go, I'll come with you,
130   And where I go, you shall come too."
"Nay, nay, dear sir, that cannot be.
I'll tell you all and then you'll see.
When I went down this morningtide
And lay disposed to sleep beside
135   Our orchard, I saw riding there
Two knights in armor, a handsome pair,
Who told me to come and have a word
Immediately with the king their lord.
But I replied that I did not dare
140   Or wish to go with them anywhere.

"They spurred away. Some minutes passed,
And then their king came, just as fast.
He brought a hundred knights or more
And lovely damosels who wore
145   Garments made from snow-white silk
And rode on steeds as white as milk.

A group of folk together more
Splendid I never saw before!
The crown upon their leader's head
150   Was not of silver or gold; instead,
Carved it was of a precious stone,
And brightly as the sun it shone.
The king took me from where I lay,
Ignoring my wishes yea or nay,
155   Lifted me onto a horse beside
His own, and ordered me to ride.
He led me through the noble gate
Of his magnificent estate
And showed me castles with high towers,
160   Rivers, forests, fields of flowers,
Horse-filled stables, barns with grain.
And then he brought me back again
And into our own orchard set me,
And with these mighty words he left me:
165   "Be sure tomorrow to be here
Beneath this impe-tree, my dear.
Then you shall go with us and live
Forevermore. But if you give
Us trouble, try to hide or dart
170   Away, you'll just be torn apart,
And that will do no good at all.
You'll still be carried to my hall
With all your limbs so badly torn
You'll wish that you had never been born!"
175   On hearing this, King Orfeo
Cried out, "Alas! Alas and woe!
Much rather would I lose my life
Than in this way my queen and wife!"
He asked advice from everyone,
180   But no one knew what could be done.

The morning found King Orfeo
Armed and mounted, ready to go.
Ten hundred knights were there with him,
Each one determined, armed and grim,
185   And then came Herodis, where she
Was called beneath the impe-tree.

They made a shield wall all the way
Around her, saying they meant to stay
And die there in the orchard green
190   Before a stranger should take their queen!
But from their midst, quite suddenly,
The queen was snatched up magically,
And that was that. No one could say
Where or how she was borne away.

195   And then such crying, tears and woe!
Back in his chamber, Orfeo
Fainted upon the floor of stone,
Then woke and let out such a moan,
He nearly killed himself with grief!
200   No one could offer him relief.
Summoned then, the barons came
And earls and lords of noble fame,
And when they had all congregated,
"Lordings, my steward here," he stated,
205   "I now, before you all, ordain
To guard you till I come again,
And rule you while I'm not around,
And keep my kingdom safe and sound.
My queen, the loveliest ever born,
210   Is gone, and lo! I am forlorn.
I'll nevermore on woman gaze,
And in the wild I'll pass my days,
Wandering there forever more
Among the hart and hare and boar.
215   And when you hear my days are spent,
Then you should call a parliament
And choose yourselves another king.
Now, do your best in everything."

Oh, then what weeping in that hall,
220   A great lament among them all!
Scarcely anyone, old or young,
Could manage words upon the tongue.
They knelt and all began to pray
Together for their king to stay,
225   To change his mind, please, and not go.

"Enough!" he said. "It must be so,"
And then his kingdom he forsook.
Only a pilgrim's cloak he took,
Neither a tunic or a hat
230   Or shirt or anything like that.
His harp he took, at any rate,
And went barefooted through the gate,
And no companion was allowed
To go with him. Then how the crowd
235   Wept when the king took off his crown
And went impoverished from the town!

Through woods and hills where heather grows
Into the wilderness he goes,
Nothing of comfort finding there.
240   He lives in sad malaise and care.
He who in ermine robes was clad
And sheets of purple linen had
Now lies upon the moss and clover,
Leaves and grasses for his cover.
245   He who had castles, mighty towers,
Rivers and forests, fields of flowers,
Now in snow and freezing weather
Makes his royal bed in heather.
He who knights and ladies had
250   Kneeling before him, sees instead
Nothing to give him joy or pride,
But just the snakes that past him glide.
He who once had much to eat
And drink, the choicest kinds of meat,
255   Now constantly must dig and root
Before he's full. On wild fruit
And summer berries he can live,
But little nourishment they give.
In winter, nothing can he find
260   But roots and grasses and the rind
Or bark of trees. Grown chapped and thin
Is now his body in every limb.
Good Lord! Such deprivation sore
This king has known ten years and more!
265   His beard has grown out black and rough

Down to his waist, and wild enough.
His harp, once so much joy, now he
Keeps hidden in a hollow tree.
But when the days are bright and clear
270   He takes it, tunes it up by ear,
And plays for pleasure, and the sound
Spills through the wilderness around.
Then all the beasts that hear that high
Sweet melody come drawing nigh,
275   And all the birds that hear him play
Come down to perch upon a spray
Of leaves to listen till it's done,
So fine it is! But then, not one
Of all those creatures thinks of staying
280   Once Orfeo has finished playing.

Now often in the woods he sees,
Bright in the mellow morning breeze,
The king of fairies with his troop
Coming to hunt. They shout and whoop
285   And blow their horns with lively sounds
And follow the barking of their hounds.
Yet never do they take their prey,
And never does he spot the way
They vanish. Other times he sees
290   A mighty host come through the trees,
Ten hundred well-accoutered knights,
Well-armed for various kinds of fights,
With faces fierce and unafraid
And many banners well displayed.
295   Their swords are drawn, but he never knows
Whither that mighty army goes.

Another time, another thing:
He sees fine ladies in a ring
Dance with knights in shining clothes,
300   With lively steps and tapping toes,
And going past are trumpets, drums—
Every kind of instrument comes.
And then he sees ride past one day
Sixty ladies on horses gay,

305　　Pretty as birds on a winter tree,
　　　　But no man with them did he see.
　　　　With hooded falcon each one rode
　　　　For hawking. Where the river flowed
　　　　Was all the game that one could want.
310　　Mallard, heron, and cormorant
　　　　Would meet, when they rose from the water,
　　　　Falcons eager for the slaughter.
　　　　When each of those falcons slew its prey,
　　　　Orfeo, seeing it, laughed. "Parfay,[8]
315　　This is," said he, "an excellent game!
　　　　I'll go and join them, in God's name.
　　　　Such sport as this I used to know."
　　　　But then, as he got up to go,
　　　　He met a lady, where she stood.
320　　He looked again, then understood
　　　　Suddenly and completely: this
　　　　Was his own lady Herodis!
　　　　Yearning, he looked. She saw him too.
　　　　Neither spoke and yet both knew.
325　　And then she let escape a sigh
　　　　To see him who had been so high
　　　　Brought low. Like rain her tears fell down.
　　　　The others saw, and with a frown
　　　　One came to make her ride away.
330　　Herodis could no longer stay.

　　　　"Alas," said Orfeo, "now I
　　　　Am truly sad. Why can't I die?
　　　　Why can I not just fall down dead
　　　　Here on the spot from which she's led?
335　　Alas, I've had too long a life
　　　　When I don't dare approach my wife,
　　　　Nor she to me. Not one word spoken!
　　　　Alas, why is my heart not broken?
　　　　But now," said he, "whatever betide,[9]
340　　Wherever those ladies choose to ride,
　　　　I shall myself go riding there.
　　　　For life or death I do not care!"

---

[8] Parfay (French): by faith (interjection).

[9] Betide: may happen.

Quickly he took his pilgrim's pack
And hung his harp upon his back,
345 And followed them where they had gone,
Hindered by neither stump nor stone.
A cave they entered in a hill
And Orfeo followed with all his will.

When in the cavern he had gone
350 Three miles or more, all slanting down,
Into a lovely land he came
Bright as the sun in summertime.
It stretched before him flat and green,
For hill or dale was nowhere seen.
355 He saw a castle by and by,
Rich and royal and wondrous high.
The outer wall was clear, and shone
As if composed of crystal stone.
The hundred towers that he could see
360 Were battlemented wonderfully.
Golden buttresses seemed to float
As they arched upward from a moat.
The vaulting was adorned and lined
With bright enamels of every kind.
365 Beyond the walls he saw, inside,
Great buildings bright with gems, and wide.
The least of the pillars to behold
Was layered over with burnished gold.
And in that land it was always light,
370 For with the coming of the night
The precious stones lit up and soon
Were shining like the sun at noon.
Nobody could begin to tell
The wealth he saw in that citadel.
375 He thought there lay before his eyes
The very courts of Paradise!

Watching the sixty ladies go
Into the castle, Orfeo
Followed and knocked at the postern gate.
380 The porters did not make him wait
But asked him what he wanted there.

"I am a minstrel," he said, "and dare
To bring your lord my songs today,
If he would like to hear me play."
385 They opened the gate for Orfeo
And into the castle they let him go.
Inside the keep's defensive wall
He saw, on looking around him, all
The folk that thither had been brought.
390 They all seemed dead—but they were not.
Some stood around without a head,
And some without their arms instead.
Some a wound through the body had,
And some lay bound, for they were mad.
395 Some were on horseback, tall and straight,
And some were strangling as they ate.
Some sank in water about to drown,
And some in fire were shriveled brown.
Some women lay there giving birth,
400 Or dying, or going mad with mirth,
And wondrous many others lay
Just as they'd slept on their final day,
Each taken from the world of men
By fairy magic and brought herein.
405 Close by he saw his own dear wife,
Dame Herodis, his love, his life,
Asleep beneath an impe-tree.
Her clothing told him it was she.
Seeing and marveling at it all,
410 He went inside the royal hall
And saw therein a seemly sight:
Within an alcove well alight
The lord their king was sitting there
Beside his lady, sweet and fair.
415 Their clothes and crowns were so aglow
They almost blinded Orfeo.

When he had gazed upon this scene,
He knelt before the king and queen.
To him he said, "Lord, if today
420 You wish, I'll show how well I play."
The king said, "What sort of man are you

Who's come so bravely hither to
Address me, when no underling
Was sent to call you here to sing?
425 In all my life I've never yet
Any mortal so hardy met
That he would dare to brave that dim
Tunnel, unless I sent for him."
"Lord," said Orfeo, "as you see,
430 I'm just a minstrel. Poor are we.
It is our custom to venture to
A noble's house, no matter who,
And though not welcome in every hall,
To offer songs to one and all."
435 Before the king he then sat down,
Unwrapped his harp, twirled pegs around
To tune it, and then skillfully
Rang out the notes so enticingly
That everyone in the neighborhood
440 Came there to hear, it was so good,
And many lay down at his feet,
The music seemed to them so sweet.
The king sat listening, very still.
To hear the music was all his will.
445 He found it charming, and to the queen
It seemed the sweetest there'd ever been.
So when the music ceased to ring,
To Orfeo announced the king:
"Minstrel, your harping pleases me,
450 So ask whatever it might be,
And generously your boon I'll grant.
Now speak, and tell me what you want."
Sir Orfeo said, "I pray you, sir,
That you would kindly grant me her,
455 That lovely lady, whom I see
Asleep beneath the impe-tree."
"Nay, nay," said the king, "that would not do.
A sorry pair you'd make, you two,
With you so dirty, rough and lean,
460 And her as gracious as a queen.
A loathsome mismatch it would be
To see you in her company."

"Oh, sir," said Orfeo, "noble king,
More loathsome far would be the thing
465   If from your mouth should come a lie.
You said just now whatever I
Might ask for, I should have from you.
A king's word always must be true."[10]
"You argue well," the king said then.
470   "You must be one of the truest men,
Therefore I grant that it be so.[11]
Take her by the hand and go.
I hope you'll be a happy pair."
Orfeo knelt and thanked him there.
475   Then taking Herodis by the hand,
He quickly went from fairyland.
He turned away and fled for home
Up the tunnel through which he'd come.

So long the two had been away
480   That nobody upon the day
That they returned to Winchester
Recognized either him or her.
Then stopping at the edge of town,
Just in case he might be known,
485   Orfeo found room in a small
Beggar's hut by the city wall
For both himself and his pretty wife.
As if a minstrel all his life,
He asked for tidings of that land
490   And if the kingdom was well in hand.
The poor old beggar told them what
He knew then, crouching in that hut:
How fairy guile ten years before
Had stolen the queen, and then the poor
495   Grief-stricken king had gone away,

---

[10] By "true" Orfeo means consistent, fair, and honest. "Truth" meaning consistency with a statement uttered earlier is a theme running through several of these romances; see, for example, the emphasis on the issue of "troth" in "The Tale of Florent."

[11] Lines 470–71 are added from manuscript Ashmole 61 for better continuity, as they provide the king with a reason to let Orfeo leave with Herodis that supplements the harper's ability to argue persuasively. This addition means, however, that subsequent line numbers will no longer correspond to editions of "Sir Orfeo" based exclusively on the Auchinleck manuscript.

And no one knew where he was today.
Then how a steward he'd left to hold
The land, and other things he told.
Orfeo asked his wife at dawn
500   To stay and wait there. He put on
A suit of borrowed rags, and put
His harp on his back, and went afoot
Into the town quite openly
To where he could be seen—and see.

505   Townsmen, earls and barons bold
And ladies stopped there to behold
Him passing by. "Just look," they said,
"How long the hair is on his head!
Look how his beard hangs to his knee!
510   He is as wrinkled as a tree!"
Then as he walked on down the street
His steward there he chanced to meet,
And with a loud cry he began
Demanding "Mercy!" from the man.
515   "A harper from heathen lands am I.
Oh, help me now, or I shall die!"
The steward said, "Come with me, come.
Of what I have, you shall have some.
Harpers are welcome here to me
520   For love of Orfeo, you see."
And then the steward went with all
His lords into the royal hall.[12]
The steward washed and went to eat,
And lords beside him took their seat.
525   They watched the blaring trumpets come
With harp and fiddle and many a drum,
And lively music was made by all.
Orfeo, silent in that hall,
Listened with ears forever sharp.
530   When all was still, he tuned his harp.
The blissfulest notes now did they hear
That ever were heard by human ear.
Everyone liked that minstrelsy.

---

[12] Lines 521–22 and part of 523 have been inserted at this point from manuscript Ashmole 61.

The steward now began to see.
535 The harp he recognized right away.
"Minstrel," he said, "you must now say
Where you acquired this harp, and how.
I pray you tell me quickly now."
"My lord," said Orfeo, "far away,
540 As in a wood I walked one day,
I came to a clearing where I found
A lion-torn man upon the ground.
Wolves were gnawing him with their sharp
Teeth, and near him lay this harp.
545 I'd say this was ten years ago."
The steward cried, "That was Orfeo,
My lord and king! I never knew
Woe before now! What shall I do,
Of such a lord bereft, forlorn?
550 Alas that I was ever born!—
That such a foul death should deface
My lord who was so marked with grace!"
He fell down then and fainted away.
The barons, raising him, had to say
555 One of those truths that all should see:
"For death there is no remedy."
But by that time King Orfeo knew
His steward faithful, always true,
Loving his lord as he ought, and so
560 He stood and spoke up loudly, "Lo!
Steward, please listen to this thing:
If I were Orfeo, your king,
And suffered long and ceaselessly
In wilderness much misery,
565 And then had won my queen away
From fairyland one summer's day,
And led her homeward, bringing her
Right to the edge of Winchester,
And took up lodging in a small
570 Beggar's hut by the city wall,
And came here in disguise to see
The scope of your good will toward me,
And if I found that you were true,
You'd never then have reason to

575   Regret the good work you had done.
        You would be king when I was gone.
        But if my death had brought you cheer,
        Quickly would you be out of here!"

        Then all those there saw it was so:
580   This was their lost king, Orfeo.
        So glad was the steward when he knew,
        He overturned tables as he flew
        Across them to his king, to fall
        Upon his knees. And so they all
585   Knelt and exclaimed in a single cry,
        "Now be our king, sir, till we die!"
        Rejoicing and glad that he was saved,
        They led him off then to be shaved
        And washed and dressed, and everything
590   Pertaining to a proper king.
        Then in procession all went down
        To welcome Herodis into town
        With every kind of minstrelsy.
        My Lord, but there was melody!
595   They wept for joy, shed many a tear
        To see their rulers reappear,
        And Orfeo was crowned anew,
        And Herodis recrowned there, too,
        And afterwards they both lived long
600   And to the steward left the throne.

        When Breton harpers came to hear
        Of this event in a later year,
        They made a pleasing tale in rhyme
        Named for this king of olden time.
605   They call it "Sir Orfeo" to this day.
        Sweet is the tune, good is the lay.
        And thus came Orfeo out of care,
        And God grant us so well to fare!
                    Amen.

Appendix: Virgil's Story
of Orpheus and Eurydice[13]

This is the same story familiar from Ovid and others, with some emphases unique to Virgil. Line numbers refer to its place in *The Georgics* (Book 4, lines 456–99). It seems that the poet is retelling a tale of which he expects his audience to know the broad outlines. The names of the mountains, peoples, and mythical beings are presented as much for their sound as for their associations. Their identity is not significant within the present context and should not be regarded as an impediment to understanding the love story. A loose pentameter blank verse has been chosen for this translation because that meter is familiar to speakers of English, yet to twenty-first-century ears it seems pleasantly archaic. (I am grateful to Emily Albu for her assistance with the Latin.)

---

[13] *The Georgics* by Virgil (Publius Vergilius Maro, 70–19 BC). Book 4 is available online, without line numbers, at <http://www.sacred-texts.com/cla/virgil/geo/geo1o4.htm>.

456   Fleeing headlong along the river, the young
    bride met her death. She never saw the snake
    deep in the grass before her feet, a watcher
    fierce on the bank. The dryads cry out across
460   the mountaintops, Rhodope, Pangaea, and Rhesus
    of Thrace, that warlike land; the Getae weep,
    and even the Hebrus, and Attic Orithyia.
    Orpheus, heartsick, found comfort in his lyre,
    alone on the shore sang "you," sang "you, sweet wife,"
465   sang "you" as dawn came, "you" at nightfall—then
    entered the chasm Taenarus, deep gate of Dis,
    the forest where fear like black mist hangs, came
    down to the spirits and that tremendous king
    and hearts not knowing the ease of human prayer.
470   Roused by his song from depths of Erebis,
    tenuous shadows, ghosts that had lost the light,
    flocked like the thousands of birds that hide among leaves
    when dusk or winter drives them from the hills;
    came mothers and men, dead bodies of heroes magnanimous
475   in life, came boys and girls as yet unmarried,
    and youths laid on pyres before their parents' eyes.
    Around them the marsh flowed black and bent reeds grew,
    the foul morass of Cocytus hemmed them in,
    and nine times wound the Styx to hold them there.
480   And those in Tartarus, inner home of Death,
    were amazed by the singing. Furies with blue snakes threading
    their hair were amazed, and Cerberus, three jaws gaping;
    and Ixion's wheel ceased its windy whirling.
    Now Orpheus, slipping all snares, is going home,
485   and *she*, restored, goes toward the upper air
    behind him—as Persephone ordained—
    when suddenly an incautious madness grips
    her lover. Forgive him? If only the dead forgave.
    He stops, his dear Eurydice a step
490   from light, alas. He forgot!—a lapse. Beaten,
    he looked behind him, lost all his labor, broke
    the pact with the merciless ruler. Thunder crashed
    thrice through Avernus' pools. "What great madness,"
    she cried, "has doomed me, poor me, and you, too—what,

495   Orpheus? They call me now, sleep shuts my eyes,
       farewell. Huge is the night around me. Helpless,
       my hands reach out to you, hands, alas, no longer
       yours ..." And at once from sight, like smoke dispersing
       in air, she was gone.

CHAPTER 5

Sir Launfal

The first thing to be aware of when reading "Sir Launfal" is that, like a graphic novel, it has its own aesthetic. Some earlier scholars who hoped for the romance form to be recognized as high literature in terms then current were appalled by this popular tale. A.J. Bliss, for example, whose 1960 edition of "Sir Launfal" remains the most complete, spends four pages of his introduction disparaging the romance's "literary value." Much of what he says is true: the lives of the characters are "strangely unreal," there is "a streak of bloodthirstiness running through the poem," Launfal is helped to victory by "unsportsmanlike intervention," and "there is no room for psychological intricacy or even accuracy" (42–45).[1] The trouble with such an assessment is

---

[1] London: Nelson, 1960. Part of this editor's problem is a desire for literal meaning. For example, when the queen declares that she has loved Launfal for seven years (clearly untrue), the knight replies in turn that he has loved his lady for seven years (line 696). Bliss objects in his note on this line, "No hint has previously been given of the passage of seven years" (96). Surely both claims should be understood to refer to intensity of passion rather than actual duration. Other such discrepancies may also be dismissed as rhetorical flourishes.

that it is mainly irrelevant for a work that is clearly intended to be fanciful and swashbuckling.

Of more interest, because more relevant, is the degree to which identity achieved through wealth and beauty is important to the characters in the story. Launfal himself is one of several destitute knights of romance who must find some means of topping up their coffers in order to regain knightly respect ("honor"). In these romances, honor depends on display even more than on valor. Though both are important for knightly identity, in "Sir Launfal" lavish giving is synonymous with courtliness (see lines 67–69, 624, etc.). Having wealth is more critical for Launfal than for others, as his identity lies mainly in his reputation for generosity, the fame of his largess matching Gawain's for courtesy. Launfal gains both wealth and success in battle through fairy intervention, and gets good sex with a beautiful partner as well. The theme of beauty is represented in this romance by both the fairy mistress and the queen, whose nymphomaniac aspect is a standard role that here is occupied by Guinevere. The queen lusts after Launfal when she sees his good looks, especially his "largess" (a pun), and the last part of the romance is wholly occupied by what we today term "the Gaze," female as well as male. Appearance, important in romance in general, is paramount in this one. The fairy Tryamour, having herself invited Launfal's gaze, warns him that she must not be revealed to others. The knight puts himself in major jeopardy when Guinevere's insult to his manhood drives him to boast of his mistress, which leads to further complications putting his life at risk. Then, despite his expectations, Dame Tryamour shows up to save him by displaying herself to the gaze of the entire court; the fairy must be judged more beautiful than the queen, and thus more worthy. To us modern readers, of course, personal worth lies in attributes more admirable than wealth and beauty—doesn't it?

Thomas Chestre, who claims "Sir Launfal" as his in the final stanza, is one of the few named authors of medieval romance. Marie de France, writing in her own language, is another, and she either invented this story or was the first to put it into written verse in her lay titled "Lanval." An unnamed poet then re-rhymed the lay in Middle English with the title "Landevale." In an extremely useful appendix to his edition of "Sir Launfal," A.J. Bliss offers Marie's story for comparison with "Landevale," so that one can see what the English author expands and deletes. Both versions are in rhymed tetrameter couplets. Chestre, changing the meter to the then more popular tail-rhyme stanza, bases his story mainly on the English "Landevale," often even using the same words (once or twice mistakenly within his own context). He also adds episodes and details, and these come mainly from two French sources: the Old French romance "Graelent" and some form of a story told by Andreas Capellanus in his *De Amore* of 1185. The long and violent episode of Sir Valentine by which Launfal establishes his reputation for valor expands a differently motivated encounter in Andreas's story, where the hero must overcome a giant guardian, as in Chaucer's "Tale of Sir Thopas."

"Sir Launfal" is the type of romance that Chaucer parodies in "Sir Thopas," aiming his mockery at the childishness of it all: the sing-songy tail-rhyme meter, the male fantasy of a fairy mistress, and the hero's giant antagonist (from whom Chaucer's Thopas sensibly runs away). All three of these are indeed clichés of the genre, and they are all present in "Sir Launfal," glaringly or amusingly, depending on your perspective. Nevertheless, as the sketch above shows, Chestre's story contains much else that may engage our interest. Not the least of these is the lively interaction between characters as they test and modify their attitudes toward each other (an aspect of "Sir Launfal" that Bliss chooses to ignore). The reader may also enjoy the more subtle punning and allusion that runs concurrently with the overt sexuality displayed in this romance.

The translation is based mainly on the 1960 edition by A.J. Bliss, with help in interpretation from other more recent editions (see bibliography). Subtitles are added by the translator.

Sir Launfal

In days when mighty Arthur was
Ruling England with good laws,
    A wondrous thing befell.
About it was composed a lay
5   That's called "Sir Launfal" to this day.
    Now listen to it well.
Mighty Arthur for a while
Went to sojourn in Carlisle,
    That joyous citadel,
10   And worthy were those assembled at
The Table Round where Arthur sat,
    Knights without parallel:

Sir Perceval and Sir Gawain,
Sir Gahéris, Sir Agravaine,
15   And Lancelot of the Lake;
Also Sir Kay and Sir Yvain,
Never known to fight in vain
    (The field they'd always take);
King Ban of Benwick and King Bors,
20   Who won great fame in Arthur's wars—
    None could their courage shake;
Sir Galafré and Sir Launfal,
And of his noble story shall
    All listeners now partake.

25   With Arthur lived a bachelor[2]
Who'd been with him ten years and more,
    And Launfal was his name.
His giving was both large and bold:
Clothing rich and silver and gold,
30   To squire and knight the same.
His lavish generosity
Was noticed, so King's Steward he

---

[2]   Bachelor: this word refers to a novice knight and has nothing to do with marriage status.

For ten long years became;[3]
For of largess,[4] none could be found
35   Of all the knights of the Table Round
    That had a better name.

Then it befell in that tenth year
That Merlin, Arthur's counselor,
    Advised the king to fare
40   To Ireland far across the water
And fetch King Ryon's noble daughter,
    The gracious Guinevere.
So this he did, but when he brought
Her home, she pleased Sir Launfal not,
45   Nor other good knights there,
Because about her spread the word
That she took lovers besides her lord
    In many an affair!

But married, as to you I say,
50   They were upon a Whitsunday[5]
    Before great men of pride.
No one alone could list and name
All those who to that wedding came
    From countries far and wide,
55   And no one in that hall could sit
Unless as prelate[6] or baronet
    His rank was verified.
Although not served according to
Their rank, good service rich and true
60   Each had on every side.

When all the lords had duly eaten,
And tablecloths were removed and beaten,
    Then, as you may hear,
The butlers served the sweet red wine

---

3 Whereas we think of a steward as someone who takes care that wealth is not squandered ("a good steward"), in King Arthur's imagined society the steward was in charge of the lavish display of wealth.

4 Largess (generosity) is a key word in this story, associated with Sir Launfal in particular.

5 Whitsunday: Pentecost (see line 133), traditionally the fiftieth day after Easter Sunday.

6 Prelate: Church official.

65　　To all those lords who came to dine,
　　　　And there was much good cheer.
　　　The queen gave many a precious stone
　　　And gold and silver to make known
　　　　Her courtliness to each peer.
70　　Each knight she gave a brooch or ring,
　　　But to Sir Launfal, not a thing!
　　　　This saddened him, I fear.

　　　So when the wedding ended, he
　　　Took his leave regretfully
75　　　From Arthur, his good king.
　　　He claimed a letter to him had come.
　　　His father had died; he must go home
　　　　To see to the burying.
　　　Then Arthur, always courteous,
80　　　Said, "Launfal, if you must go from us,
　　　　Take money for everything
　　　You need, and take my sister's two
　　　Sons, my nephews, along with you
　　　　For the accompanying."

85　　Then Launfal took leave of every knight
　　　Of the Table Round, as was polite,
　　　　And traveled until he
　　　Arrived in Caerleon[7] at the house
　　　Of the city's mayor, he who was
90　　　His servant previously.
　　　The mayor, when he saw him ride
　　　At easy pace, with at his side
　　　　Knights in his company,
　　　Went out and met him on his way
95　　And said, "Sir knight, you are welcome! Say,
　　　　How fares our king? Tell me!"

7　　Pronounced CARE-lee-on, in three syllables with stress on the first. This town near modern
　　Cardiff in Wales lies about 300 miles south of Carlisle. Late in the story the author seems to
　　get confused about whether his action is located in Caerleon or Carlisle.

Sir Launfal answered, saying then,
"He fares as well as any man,
   Or it would be too bad.
100   But, look, Sir Mayor, I will not lie:
We are estranged, the king and I.
   This makes me very sad,
For no one, now, need give me honor,
High or low, for their love of Arthur.
105   Therefore, I'd be glad,
Sir Mayor, with you, if I may,
Along with my companions, stay,
   For friendship we once had."

The mayor stood and thought a while
110   Of what to say, then with a smile
   "I must explain," said he.
"Some knights have taken in my home
Lodging, and they soon will come,
   Seven, from Brittany."
115   Sir Launfal turned away to laugh—
For those words he had scorn enough.
   "Young knights," he said, "Now see
How dedicated service is
Under a lord who's valueless—
120   How pampered he may be!"

But when he turned to ride away,
The mayor called to him to stay,
   And spoke as you may hear:
"Sir, there's a chamber out beside
125   My orchard where, if you wish, with pride,
   You may be lodged, quite near."
Launfal accepted, both for him
And his two knights. The three of them
   Then lived together there,
130   But so extravagantly he spent
His money that into debt he went
   Within that very year.

Then it befell at Pentecost
(Around the time the Holy Ghost
135   Chose dove-like to descend[8])
That Arthur's nephews Hugh and John
Decided that they must be gone
From Sir Launfal, their friend.
"Our clothes are torn," they said. "We're clad
140   Like paupers, and of the wealth you had,
You have no more to spend."[9]
Sir Launfal said then, "For the love
Of God, do not tell others of
The way my fortunes tend."

145   The two young knights had this to say:
That neither ever would betray
Their friend for anything in
The world. And so they left him there
And went to Glastonbury, where
150   King Arthur was, and when
The king perceived each noble youth
He hastened toward them, for in truth
They were of his own kin.
With them they had no other clothes
155   But what they'd left in. Truly those
Were tattered and quite thin—

So then said Guinevere spitefully,
"The proud knight Launfal, how is he?
And arms can he still bear?"
160   "Oh, yes, madam, of course he can,
And just as well as any man,
God willing, does he fare."
They spoke then of his high esteem
Both to King Arthur and the queen,
165   And said he was happy where
He lived. "However, he loved us so,
He did not wish to see us go
And wanted to keep us there.

---

[8]   The event is described in Acts 2 in the New Testament.

[9]   It is Launfal's duty to clothe his followers properly, and now he cannot do so.

"One rainy day, it so befell

170   That we went hunting with Sir Launfal
      In wilderness old and hoar,[10]
And wore old clothes to suit the weather.
Then we decided to come, together,
      In just the clothes we wore."

175   The king was very glad to hear
Sir Launfal's news, but Guinevere
      Was not so happy, for
She had desired with all her might
That he should suffer day and night

180   In sorrow more and more.

Upon the day of the Trinity,[11]
A feast of great solemnity
      Was held in Caerleon.
Earls and barons of high rank came,

185   And ladies and burgesses[12] of the same
      Were there, both old and young.
But Launfal, since he had no money,
Was not invited to that assembly;
      No longer did he belong.

190   They did invite the mayor, who
Attended. Then his daughter to
      Sir Launfal went along

And said she hoped he'd dine that day
With her, but he said, "Damsel, nay,

195   I have no spirit for
Dining, though for three days, I think,
I have not tasted meat or drink,
      Because I am so poor.
To church today I would have gone

200   Had I good clothing to put on,
      Clean shirt and breeches, for
To go in wretched clothes among
A crowd of worshippers would be wrong.
      No wonder my heart is sore!

---

[10] Hoar: gray.

[11] Trinity Sunday falls on the next Sunday after Pentecost.

[12] Burgess: city dweller. (Burg: city.)

205 But damsel, for one thing I pray:
Lend me saddle and bridle today
    So I can go and ride
For comfort far away from town
This sunny morning, up and down
210   The open countryside."
Launfal harnessed the damsel's horse
Himself (having no squire, of course),
    And rode with little pride.
And then his horse slipped in the fen,
215 And all around him many men
    Were laughing, far and wide.

The poor knight sadly mounted up.
Meaning to make the staring stop,
    He rode into the west.
220 That day the weather was so hot
That near a forest Launfal thought
    He'd pause to take a rest.
Then he removed, in all that heat,
His cape and folded it, nice and neat,
225   And now less warmly dressed,
The knight, in his simplicity,[13]
Sat in the shadow of a tree
    Whose comfort seemed the best.

As mournfully he rested there,
230 Among the trees he saw a pair
    Of maidens come his way.
Their silken gowns of India-blue
Were tightly laced, and never were two
    More gaily dressed than they.
235 Their mantles of green velvet were,
Bordered with gold and lined with fur
    Of alternate white and gray.[14]

---

[13] Simplicity: i.e., not formally clad.

[14] The text says "gris and gro," which refers specifically to the two colors of the pelt of a northern species of squirrel, having bluish-gray fur on the back and white on the stomach. This patterned fur, found throughout romance where it is sometimes called "ver," is designated "vair" in heraldry. The harlequined vair is one of the two main furs associated with heraldry; the other is ermine. See line 329 below for the lady's ermine coat-of-arms.

Their hair was held in a golden net,
And each was wearing a coronet
240   Of sixty gemstones gay.

Their skin was pale as snow on the down,[15]
Complexions rosy, eyes of brown,
     And truly never did I
See fairer! One a golden basin
245 Bore for the knight to wash his face in,
     The other, a towel to dry.
The kerchiefs were heavy that they wore
With threads of gold, compelling poor
     Launfal sadly to sigh.
250 They came to him across the heath.
Politely he rose and stood beneath
     The tree as they drew nigh.

"Damsels," he said, "God cherish you!"
"Sir knight," they said, "God bless you, too!
255   "Dame Tryamour today,
Requests that you come speak with her,
If it would be your pleasure, sir,
     Without the least delay."
Launfal consented courteously
260 And followed those maidens fair to see,
     As fresh as flowers in May,
And as they came into the wood
He saw where a pavilion stood,
     Magnificent and gay.

265 Saracens[16] had designed that tent
And all its lovely ornament.
     Its crystal pommels[17] shone.
Upon the apex an eagle stood,

---

[15] Down: hillside.

[16] Saracens (Muslims) are the great artificers of medieval fantasy, sometimes replaced by fairies or Jews, and the gems they contrive to pour out light after dark are a standard motif, found, for example, here in "Sir Launfal," in "Sir Orfeo," in "Floris and Blancheflour," and elsewhere as well. In "Landevale" the tent is topped with a heron holding in its beak the ruby (carbuncle) that pours out light; Marie's earlier version has a ruby-eyed eagle here.

[17] Pommels: the knobs at the ends of the tent-poles.

Of burnished goldwork, rich and good,
270   Enamel too, and bone.
His eyes were rubies that gleamed as bright
As does the moon that shines at night,
     And better jewels had none:
Not even Alexander the Great
275 Or Arthur, king and potentate,
     Regal upon his throne!

Under that canopy, Sir Launfal
Found her of Olyroun[18] whom they call
     Dame Tryamour by right.
280 The king her father was a fairy
Who lived far in the west, and there he
     Ruled with royal might.
Inside the tent there was a bed.
A linen coverlet it had
285   Of purple, a noble sight,
And thereupon the lady fair
Who had invited Launfal there
     Lay glittering and bright.

For coolness, far down she had cast
290 Her garment nearly to her waist
     And lay uncovered there.
Her skin was white as a lily in May
Or snow that falls on a winter's day.
     He'd never seen woman so fair.
295 The pinkest rose when it is new
Would fade against her cheeks' warm hue.
     The fan of her long hair
Shone bright as threads of golden wire.
As for describing her attire,
300   No one would even dare.

"Sir Launfal, noble knight, hereby,"
She said, "all other loves do I
     Renounce, my paramour!
I love no one in a Christian land

---

[18]   Olyroun: Marie de France identifies this place as Avalon.

305 So much as I love you, my friend,
   Not king or emperor!"
 When on her fell Sir Launfal's gaze,
 He knew he'd love her all his days,
   The beautiful Tryamour.
310 He kissed her, sitting at her side,
   And said, "Sweetheart, whatever betide,
    I'm yours forevermore."

 And then she said, "Sir gracious knight,
 I'm well aware of your sad plight.
315   Don't be ashamed with me.
 If other women you'll forsake
 And as your paramour will take
   No other love but me,
 I'll make you rich. A silken purse
320 With trim of gold I'll give you first,
   Adorned with images three.
 Each time you reach within, you'll hold
 A newly-minted coin of gold,
   Wherever you might be.

325 "And then," she said, "to you, Launfal,
 I'll give my steed Blanchard as well.
   You'll have Gifré, my knave.[19]
 My coat-of-arms on a pennon, too,
 With ermines three on field of blue,[20]
330   This you shall also have,
 And nothing in tournament or fight
 Can injure you, no blow of knight.
   Thus I'm prepared to save
 My knight." He thanked her gallantly
335 And said, "No better security
   Could I, sweet lady, have!"

---

[19] Gifré: pronounced Gif-RAY. Knave: servant.

[20] A pennon (pensel) is a type of banner bearing an identifying heraldic device. The knight
  wearing this in battle would proclaim his allegiance to a particular lady or party. (The
  translator has added "blue" for the rhyme. This color is not specified in the original, but see
  the messengers' livery at line 385.)

The damsel now sat up and told
Her maids to bring her the basin of gold
To wash in. Then was spread
340   A cloth on the table without delay,
Then supper was served, and to it they
Went, and well were fed.
Ample was both the food and wine,
With from the Valley of the Rhine
345   A spiced and honeyed red.
When they had supped and day was over,
Sir Launfal and his fairy lover
Went at once to bed.

With playing,[21] little they slept that night.
350   She bade him rise, though, when the light
Of day began to dawn.
"Sir knight, if ever you wish to speak
To me," she said, "then you must seek
A place to be alone,
355   And I shall come so secretly
That no one alive will notice me—
As still as any stone."[22]
Then was Sir Launfal glad, and so
He kissed her many times in a row.
360   (How often is not known.)

"But knight," she said, "I caution you:
Boasting of me you must not do,
No matter what the goad,
For if you do, just so you'll know,
365   You'll lose my love by doing so!"
(Trouble such words forebode.)
When Launfal took his leave, Gifré
Brought his horse out right away;
His usefulness he showed.
370   Sir Launfal leaping then upon
The borrowed saddle, back to town
In his poor clothing rode.

---

21   Playing: having sex. (Cp. modern English "foreplay.")

22   A frequent simile in medieval romance, meaning "very quietly."

Then was his heart at ease at last,
And in his chamber Launfal passed
    The rest of the peaceful day.

375

There came then through the city ten
Well-armored and well-mounted men
    In whose horse-panniers lay
Bags of silver, bags of gold,

380 And all for Sir Launfal the bold.
    Also a fine array
Of clothes they brought and armor bright.
They asked whose house Launfal the knight
    Had chosen for his stay.

385 The messengers, all clad blue,
Rode first. Gifré then rode there too,
    On Blanchard, white as snow.
A boy who in the market stood
Said, "Tell us, friend, to whom these good

390   Treasures are meant to go."
Gifré replied, "These things have all
Been sent as gifts to Sir Launfal,
    Who has endured much woe."
Then said the boy, "He's but a wretch,

395 And who would want to deal with such?
    He's at the mayor's, though."

So to the mayor's house they went
With all the treasures that were meant
    For Launfal, whereupon

400 The mayor, seeing that vast wealth
And Launfal's status, felt himself
    Deceived and put upon.
He said to him, "For charity,
Sir, come today to dine with me!

405   Yesterday afternoon
I went to ask if you'd like to go
With me to enjoy the feast, but lo!
    You had already gone."

"Sir Mayor, God love you! When did you,
410   When I was poor, think ever to
        Invite me in to dine?
Now I have more in property
That my good friends have sent to me
        Than you and all of thine!"
415   The mayor left in shame. The knight
Then dressed in purple trimmed with white
        Ermine in the design.
All he had borrowed heretofore
Gifré repaid it, that and more:
420   Both principal and fine.

Launfal began to hold great feasts.
He first fed fifty starving guests
        Who out-of-pocket were.
For fifty he bought handsome steeds,
425   For fifty met the clothing-needs
        Of penniless knight and peer,
Rewarded fifty ministers,
Paid debts for fifty prisoners
        To make them free and clear,
430   And fifty minstrels then he clad,
And equal honors to many had
        Soon done, both far and near.

Now all the lords of Caerleon sent
Announcements of a tournament
435   For love of Sir Launfal.
(They also wished to appraise his steed,
To see how well he would succeed,
        Standing so fine and tall.)
And when was come the scheduled day,
440   Out rode the knights in fine array
        With trumpeters, who all
Raised horns at once and gaily blew
As other lords came into view
        That rode from the citadel.

445   And then the tournament began,
        And each knight at another ran
            With swords and maces both.
        A person might see courses run
        Where steeds were lost and others won,
450   And knights were nothing loath.
        Since first was made the Table Round,
        No better tournament could be found,
           I dare well say, forsooth![23]
        Many a lord of Caerleon
455   Was felled in his habergeon.[24]
           On this I take my oath.

        The constable of Caerleon
        Rode at Launfal, big and strong,
           Unable to abide
460   The waiting. When he struck at him,
        The knight struck back, then fast and grim
           Were blows on either side.
        But Launfal, of the two more wary,
        Bore him out of his saddle, where he
465   Fell and lost his pride.
        Gifré then leapt invisibly
        Onto the constable's horse, and he
           Away began to ride.

        The Earl of Chester, seeing this,
470   Became so angry that, hit or miss,
           He rode hard to assail
        Sir Launfal, struck his helmet high,
        Sliced at the crest and made it fly!
           (Thus says, in French, the tale.)
475   Launfal was very strong indeed.
        He turned and knocked him off his steed
           In all his shining mail.
        But then around Launfal amassed
        Knights of Wales in numbers so vast
480   That anyone would quail.

---

[23] Forsooth: in truth, but it is usually a meaningless filler expression, as here.

[24] Habergeon: breast armor.

And then what shields one could see splitting,
What spears that broke when thrust, what hitting
    From both behind and before!
Through blows by Launfal and his steed,
485   Many a knight was made to bleed
    And struck down in his gore!
And so the prize of the tournament
That day to noble Launfal went
    Without the least demur.
490   He rode to the house in Caerleon
Owned by the mayor of that town,
    And many lords rode before.

Then Sir Launfal, the knight so noble,
Held a feast so rich his table
495   Was for a fortnight full.
The earls and barons who attended
Were richly clothed and very splendid,
    Frolicking in that hall.
And Tryamour came every day
500   To Launfal's chamber, where she'd stay
    The entire night. Of all
Those folk who were around there then,
No one saw her but these two men:
    Gifré and Sir Launfal.

The Episode of Sir Valentine

505   A knight there was in Lombardy[25]
Who envied Launfal mightily.
    Sir Valentine was his name.
He'd heard folk speak of Sir Launfal,
Of how he jousted best of all,
510   A man of might and fame.
Sir Valentine was wondrous strong.
His body was fifteen feet long,
    And he was quite aflame
With his desire to meet the knight
515   Sir Launfal in a joust or fight,
    Just these two in the game.

---

[25] Lombardy: a province of Italy.

And so Sir Valentine had them call
A messenger into his hall.
 He told him that he would
520 Be sent to Britain, to find the knight
Reputed to have superior might
 As quickly as he could.
"And say, for the sake of his lady-love,
In order on the field to prove
525 Her courtliness, he should
Come here to me at once to joust
To keep his armor free from rust,
 Or lose manhood[26] for good!"

The messenger went forth dutifully
530 To do his lord's command, and he
 Had excellent winds to waft
Him over the sea. When he had come
To where Sir Launfal was at home,
 He said on his lord's behalf,
535 "Good sir, my lord sent me to you—
Sir Valentine, a warrior who
 Is skillful in his craft—
To ask you, for your lady's sake,
If you a joust with him would take."
540 Then Launfal quietly laughed,

And said, since he was a noble knight,
He'd come to him on the fourteenth night
 With Valentine to play,
And to the messenger sent to bring
545 The challenge, he gave a horse and ring,
 And then a robe of ray.[27]
Launfal took leave of his lady fair,
Dame Tryamour, in his chamber where
 He kissed that lady gay.
550 Then said that maiden fair and sweet,
"Don't fear a thing when you two meet.
 You'll slaughter him on that day!"

---

[26] Lose manhood: i.e., lose his reputation for valor, but compare lines 689 and 775 for another meaning.

[27] Ray: a special kind of silk.

Launfal decided he'd only need
His squire Gifré and Blanchard his steed,
 So with these companions he
555 Sailed away, and winds were good,
Driving them over the salty flood
 And on to Lombardy.
When over the ocean he had come
560 To where Sir Valentine was at home
 (The city of Atalye),[28]
He found him with a mighty host,
But Launfal soon would cool their boast
 With his small company.

565 And when on Blanchard, light[29] but steady,
Sir Launfal was prepared and ready
 With helmet, spear and shield,
All who saw him in armor bright
Agreed that never was such a knight
570 To mortal eyes revealed.
Together then these two knights dashed
So violently that their lances crashed
 And shattered on the field.
And then another course they rode
575 So hard that from his head, it's told,
 Sir Launfal's helmet peeled!

Sir Valentine laughed and thought it fun.
Such shame to Launfal had never been done
 Before, in any fight.
580 Gifré then showed his use in need.
He leapt upon his master's steed,
 And nobody saw that sight.
The second time the two knights met,
On Launfal's head Gifré had set
585 The helmet, firm and tight.
Then was Sir Launfal glad indeed.
He thanked Gifré (still on his steed)
 For putting things to right.

---

28 Atalye: an imaginary city, but cp. "Italy."

29 Light: i.e., light-footed.

Valentine then struck Launfal's shield
590 So hard it tumbled toward the field,
But quickly, with a bound,
Gifré had grabbed it by the rim
And handed it back up to him
Before it hit the ground.
595 So Launfal gladly spurred his horse
And rode again in a final course,
A knight of much renown.
He struck Sir Valentine on the head
And man and warhorse both fell dead,
600 So heartily did he pound.

The lords of Atalye were all
Furious then at Sir Launfal
For Valentine being gone.
They swore the British knight would be
605 Dead before leaving Atalye;
They'd have him hanged and drawn.[30]
Sir Launfal forth his falchion[31] drew
And cutting them down as light as dew
Had soon wreaked havoc on
610 All of those lords of Lombardy.
Then back to Britain joyfully
He went, for he had won.

When mighty Arthur got the news
About the noble Launfal, whose
615 Courage was manifest,
A summons he sent him to come home
For St. John's Mass,[32] for he was known
Now for great noblesse;[33]
And he, King Arthur, planned to hold
620 A feast for earls and barons bold,

---

[30] An established ritual: first the felon would be hanged, then the body drawn apart by horses.

[31] Falchion: technically, a short, broad, slightly curved sword, but often merely a non-specific synonym for "sword." In the romance titled "Sir Gowther" the term seems to have the more specific meaning.

[32] St. John's Mass: June 24.

[33] Noblesse (French): nobility, as in the modern borrowed phrase in English, "noblesse oblige," the responsibility of those with wealth and power to care for those having less.

And all lords great and less.[34]
He wanted as steward Sir Launfal
To supervise, delighting all
    Who came with his largess.

625   So Launfal took leave of Tryamour
To go now to King Arthur for
    The task that he should do.
He found there much nobility:
Ladies beautiful to see
630   And knights of valor, too.
For forty days the feast would last,
Royal with riches unsurpassed.
    (And why should I lie to you?)[35]
The guests upon the fortieth day
635   Took their leave and went away,
    Each with his retinue.

Then after dinner Sir Gawain,
Sir Gaheres, Sir Agravain,
    And Sir Launfal also,
640   Went out to dance upon the green
Close by the tower where the queen
    Was sitting. Those below
Chose Sir Launfal to lead the rest
In dancing, loved for his largess.
645   In this it resulted, though:
The queen leaned out and watched them all.
"I see," she said, "dance large Launfal;
    To him I wish to go.

"Of all the knights that I see there,
650   He is the bachelor most fair,
    Yet never had a wife.
Betide me good, betide me ill,[36]
Down I'll go and find out his will.
    I love him like my life!"
655   She took with her as company

---

34 Less: i.e., lower in rank.

35 Why should I lie to you?: a typical filler line.

36 Betide me good, betide me ill: for better or worse.

The fairest ladies she could see,
    Sixty ladies and five.
As they went down to dance with all
The knights, she glided toward Sir Launfal
660   Without appearing to strive.

She went to the upper end between
Gawain and Launfal. Behind the queen
    Came all her ladies bright,
And all went dancing in a row.
665   To see them was a pretty show,
    A lady to each knight.
Among the many minstrels were
Fiddler, citoler,[37] trumpeter,
    For less would not be right,
670   And there they danced, it's true to say,
The rest of that long summer day,
    Till it was nearly night.

When joy of dancing began to pall,
Then did the queen approach Launfal
675   And spoke as you shall hear:
"Now for the longest time, sir knight,
You I have loved with all my might—
    This is the seventh year!
Unless you love me equally,
680   I'll surely die for love of thee,
    Launfal, my lemman[38] dear."
To this replied the noble knight,
"I'll be no traitor by day or night,
    By God, to a king I revere!"[39]

685   She said, "Oh, then, you coward, fie!
You should be hanged both hard and high!
    A pity your mother bore
    A coward, let you grow up, too!

---

[37] Citoler: a player of the medieval guitar-like stringed instrument called a citole or cittern.

[38] Lemman: beloved, sweetheart.

[39] To have an affair with a queen counts as being not only an adulterer but a traitor because of the danger of producing an illegitimate heir to the throne. This would affect not only the husband but the nation as well, so it is a greater crime than adultery.

You love no woman and no woman you!
690　　　You ought to die, therefore!"
The knight was sorely shamed and so
To answer back could not forgo
　　In words he'd be sorry for:
"I've loved a fairer woman than
695　　You've ever laid your eyes upon,
　　　For seven years and more!"

"Her ugliest maid would better be
A queen than you," then added he,
　　"In all your life!" Then red
700　　Went Queen Guenivere in her fury.
She called her maidens all to hurry
　　And back to her tower fled.
She went to bed, pulled up the cover,
And swore, before five days were over,
705　　　If she survived, she said,
She'd be so avenged on Sir Launfal
That just as harshly one and all
　　　Would speak of him, instead.

Back from his hunt returned the king,
710　　Relaxed and happy with everything,
　　　Then went to his room, where he
Encountered the queen, who began to cry:
"Avenge me, or I shall surely die!
　　　My heart will break in three![40]
715　　I spoke to Launfal just in play,
And he said to my shame today
　　　His lover I should be,
And then of another this boast he made:
The ugliest maid his lover had
720　　　Would better be queen than me!"

So angry was Arthur that he proclaimed,
"By God, Sir Launfal should be slain!"
　　　And then he called upon
Four doughty knights. To them the king

---

[40]　In three: a standard phrase for a breaking heart.

725 Ordered that Launfal they should bring
  To have him hanged and drawn.
 Quickly they went to seek him whom
 The king demanded, but to his room
  He'd gone to be alone.
730 He sought his love, but she was lost,
 As she had warned would be the cost.
  His happiness was gone!

 He looked into his purse for money
 Where he so often had found plenty
735 Whenever he had need,
 But none was there, it's sad to say.
 Gifré had also gone away
  On Blanchard, his good steed.
 Now all that previously he'd won
740 Melted like snow beneath the sun,
  As in the romance we read.
 His armor that was lily-white
 Had now become as black as night,
  And Launfal was sad indeed.

745 "Alas," he said, as he thought of her,
 "Without you, how can I endure,
  Beloved Tryamour?
 All joy is lost—but loss of thee,
 That is the worst of all for me,
750 Thou blissful maid!" Therefore,
 He beat his body and his head
 And cursed the mouth with which he'd said
  Those words that made him sore
 With sorrow, then he tumbled down,
755 And in a swoon he hit the ground,
  Just as came in the door

 The knights, who bound and made him go
 (And this brought Launfal further woe)
  Before the mighty king.
760 Then said King Arthur to him, "I
 Cannot, foul traitor, fathom why
  You'd boast of such a thing.

To say your lover's ugliest maid
Was fairer than my wife betrayed
765   You in a foul slandering!
And you had asked her, even before
That boast, to be your paramour,
    An arrogant love-making!"

Standing there, the knight replied
770 Angrily that the queen had lied
    In claiming that, for he
"Never," he said, "in all my life
Would proposition the queen your wife
    To any such foolery!
775 But she said I was not a man
And that I loved no woman, and
    Scorned women's company.
I thought of my lady, and I said
That worthier was her ugliest maid
780   To be a queen than she.

"And this, my lords, is really true!
And I am ready now to do
    Whatever will make you look
To see the truth, that I am right."
785 Of twelve now gathered, every knight
    Was sworn upon the Book,[41]
And then they whispered there between
Themselves how well they knew the queen,
    And enquiry undertook,
790 And of the queen there was the word
That she took lovers besides her lord,
    Which none could overlook.

Therefore in this they, one and all,
Judged the queen guilty, not Launfal.
795   From that charge he was clear.
Then if he brought the woman he
Had boasted of, and her maids or she
    Lovelier did appear
Than Lady Guinevere the queen,

---

[41]   The Book: the Bible. Swearing on the Bible to testify truly was a form still used until recently in American and British courtrooms as well as for official swearing-in ceremonies.

800   Why, then, Sir Launfal should be seen
          As also truthful here.
      If he could not, though, as a thief[42]
      They'd hang him in their disbelief
          For slandering Guinevere.

805   And so they formally proposed
      That Launfal's lover should be disclosed,
          And this he pledged to do.
      Then said Queen Guinevere, "If he
      A fairer woman can bring than me,
810   Put out my eyes[43] of blue!"
      When on their condition the court agreed,
      They said that Sir Launfal would need
          Of guarantors only two,
      So Sir Gawain and Sir Perceval
815   Together swore that Sir Launfal
          Would come when he was due.

      The day that they assigned, I hear,
      Was thence a fortnight and a year.
          They gave him this time to bring
820   His lover there. But Launfal then,
      Knowing his hope was pretty thin,
          His hands began to wring,
      And such despair then fell upon
      The knight, he'd gladly have foregone
825   His life, in sorrowing,
      For there was nothing he could do.
      Everyone else was sorry, too,
          Who knew about that thing.

      The day assigned was drawing near.
830   His guarantors brought Sir Launfal where

---

[42] As a thief: for devaluing her? For "stealing" her reputation? Or would they merely hang him *like* a thief?

[43] Put out my eyes!: an interjection indicating disbelief and having no more literal meaning than today's "Break a leg!" (or "Damn my eyes!"), but her idle exclamation has a repercussion later in the story.

The king would testify.[44]
They said he should bring his lady now.
Launfal replied he did not know how,
    And deeply did he sigh.
835 The king then told the barons all
To pass their judgment on Launfal,
    Condemning him to die.
The Earl of Cornwall to the king
Said, "We will *not* do such a thing,
840   And here's the reason why—

"It would dishonor us to condemn
To death a nobleman like him,
    A generous vavasour.[45]
So therefore, lords, heed what I say!
845 We wish to proceed another way:
    The land let him abjure!"[46]
And as they stood around deciding,
The barons saw ten maidens riding,
    And each was lovelier
850 Than was the last. And it was seen
By all, that worthy to be a queen
    Even the ugliest were.

Gawain to Launfal courteously
Said, "Brother, you need not worry. See,
855   Here comes your lady dear!"
"Gawain, my friend," Launfal replied,
"I do not see my lady ride
    Among those coming here."
To the castle they rode in state
860 And then dismounted at the gate
And bowed when they drew near
The king. They told him to make ready
A chamber for their noble lady,
    Appropriate to her.

---

44 Testify: Bliss suggests this word as giving the best sense of *recordede*: "Since, in the absence
of the queen, who naturally does not appear [to give public testimony], the king is the only
witness against Launval" (99).

45 Vavasour: a landholder ranking below a baron but holding vassals under himself.

46 Land let him abjure: go into exile.

865   "Who is your lady?" Arthur said.
          "You will find out, sir," said a maid,
               For here she is soon to ride."
          The king commanded them to take
          The nicest chamber, for her sake,
870   Of all the rooms inside,
          Then for his barons sent, each one
          To give his final judgment on
              That traitor full of pride.
          The barons answered firmly, "We
875   Must first of all the maidens see,
              And then we will decide."

          They went on then debating, though,
          Some for well and some for woe,
             To please their lord the king.
880   Some condemned Sir Launfal there,
          And some absolved him, fair and square,
             All fiercely arguing.
          But then they saw another ten
          Fair maidens coming, fairer than
885   The first, if anything.
          Each rode a pretty mule of Spain
          With saddle and bridle from Champagne,[47]
            And harness glittering.

          In silken gown each one was clad,
890   And everyone who saw them had
             A great desire to stare.
          Sir Gawain said, that courteous knight,
          "Sir Launfal, here must come the right
             Sweet lady to ease your care."
895   Sir Launfal sadly responded, though,
          "Alas, not one of them do I know
             Among the ladies there."
          The maidens rode up to the palace
          Then dismounted before the dais
900   And Arthur in his chair.

---

[47] Champagne: a region in France.

They greeted him, and Guinevere too,
And one of the maids stepped forward, who
   Spoke thus to mighty Arthur:
"Prepare your hall and hide the walls
905   With tapestries and sumptuous palls;[48]
   My lady comes at her leisure."
"You're welcome here," the king decreed,
"Maidens most beautiful indeed,
   By Our Lord God the Savior!"
910   He bade Sir Lancelot take them where
The rest of their companions were,
   With honor and much pleasure.

By now the queen suspected guile,
That Launfal would be, in but a while,
915   Acquitted of all blame
By his fair lady, drawing nigh.
And so she said to Arthur, "My
   Lord, if you loved your name
And cared enough about your honor,
920   You would avenge me on that traitor
   Who makes me blush with shame.
Do not spare him as your barons would,
Who humiliate you for his good,
   He is so dear to them!"

The Lady

925   As thus the queen spoke to the king,
The barons saw come cantering[49]
   A damsel all alone.
She rode a pretty horse, and they
Had never seen so fair and gay
930   A lady of blood and bone.
Lovely she was as bird on the wing
And fair enough in everything
   To dwell in an earthly home,

---

[48] Pall: a rich, heavy fabric.

[49] Canter: a smooth and easy horse's gait (see line 928).

And bright as a briar blossom too,
935   Expression charming, eyes of blue,
          And like a light she shone.

Her cheeks were rosy, and her hair
Was shining on her head as fair
          As gold wire shimmering bright.
940   She had a crown upon her head
Of gold studded with gems. It's said
          They shone with a lovely light.
The lady was clad in purple pall.
Her shape was noble, her waist was small
945   And seemly to the sight.
Lined was the cloak enwrapping her
With the most elegant ermine fur,
          Thick and rich and white.

Her saddle, the finest ever seen,
950   Was set on a velvet blanket, green
          And painted with imagery.
The hem was hung with little bells
Made of pure gold and nothing else
          That anyone could see.
955   Upon the saddle bows there shone,
On front and back, a precious stone
          Of India, gloriously.
The armor on her horse's breast,
Worth an earldom, was of the best
960   They make in Lombardy.

She bore a falcon on her hand.
A gentle pace her palfrey[50] found,
          So all there could behold.
Through Caerleon they saw her ride
965   With two white greyhounds by her side
          With collars of bright gold.
When Launfal saw that lady fair,
He shouted out to everyone there,
          Both the young and old:

---

[50] Palfrey: a horse bred specifically for gentle riding.

970   "Here now I see my lady come,
And if she wants, she can save me from
    Misfortunes manifold!"

Forth she went into the hall
Where sat the queen with her ladies all.
975   The king was also there.
Her maidens came, as they were wont,[51]
To take her stirrup to help dismount
    Dame Tryamour the fair.
She let her cloak slip to the floor
980   So all upon her beauty more
    Effectively could stare.
Then forward came the king to greet
The lady, who replied with sweet
    Language debonair.

985   Up came the queen with her retinue
To gaze upon the lady, who
    Stood elegant and polite.
By hers, their beauty faded away
As does the moon by the sun by day
990   When dawn comes bringing light.
She spoke then to the mighty king:
"Sir, I have come for just one thing,
    To clear Launfal the knight.
For never did he, in folly vain,
995   Seek to seduce your lady queen,
    Either by day or night.

"Take heed now, King, though the truth be grim:
He asked not her, but she asked him
    That lover he should be.
1000   And he replied to her and said
That his beloved's ugliest maid
    Was fairer than was she."
King Arthur then replied, "Forsooth,
Any may see that is the truth:
1005   You're lovelier than is she."

---

[51] Wont: accustomed.

With that, Dame Tryamour went to
The queen, and such a breath she blew
    That never more could she see.[52]

And then the lady said good day
1010   And leapt on her horse to ride away,
    And from the forest side
Gifré came with the utmost speed
Bringing to the knight his steed
    Where Launfal stood aside.
1015   The knight sprang on his back at once,
And away without a backward glance
    Did he with his lady ride.
Dame Tryamour with her maidens fair
Returned the way she had come there,
1020   Cheerfully and with pride.

The lady rode through old Carlisle,[53]
Then far away to the fairy isle
    Called Olyroun the bright,
And every year on a certain day
1025   One can hear Launfal's charger neigh
    And see him with clear sight.
Whoever wants may ask a joust
To keep his armor free from rust,
    In tournament or fight.
1030   Although the man may never dare
To go in farther, he'll find there
    A joust with Launfal the knight.

Thus was Launfal, once a noble
Knight of King Arthur's famous Table
1035   Taken by a fairy. He
Has not been seen by human eye

---

[52] See line 810.

[53] Here and again at line 1040 Thomas follows his source "Landevale" inattentively. Previously he has situated most of the action of his romance in King Arthur's southern court at Caerleon in Wales, and there is no hint that the court has now moved back north (see line 964). The names Caerleon and Carlisle are easy enough to confuse if one is not thinking geographically.

Since then,[54] and there is no more I
    Can tell you truthfully.
Thomas Chestre made this tale
1040   About the noble Sir Launfale,[55]
    A knight of chivalry.
May Jesus, Heaven's king, give us
His blessing high, and also thus
    His mother Saint Marie.
           —Amen!

---

[54] This is a direct contradiction of the previous stanza.

[55] Launfale: after calling him "Launfal" as recently as at lines 1032 and 1033, thus the poet names his hero here, perhaps for the rhyme with "tale."

CHAPTER 6

Sir Thopas

"Sir Thopas"—the name refers to the gemstone topaz—is the tale that Geoffrey Chaucer has his not-too-bright projected persona tell in *The Canterbury Tales* on the pilgrimage to Canterbury. (Line numbers correspond to those in *The Riverside Chaucer*, locating this tale within Fragment VII of *The Canterbury Tales*.) This pilgrim narrator and inept poet should not be confused with the brilliant Chaucer who is author of the *Tales*. Despite what our pilgrimage "Host" says at the end, when he so rudely cuts off Chaucer for too "drasty" rhyming (line 923—the real Chaucer being the greatest medieval rhymer of them all), this tale is a perfect match for the Chaucer within the *Tales*. With its galloping meter and similarly galloping plot, it is in fact a brilliant parody of the genre of tail-rhyme romance, especially the chivalric romance featuring a heroic knight on a quest.

The parody takes various forms and addresses various romance clichés. Among these are the meter, of course; the pretty-boy appearance of the knight and his falling in love at the drop of a hat, or in this case the warbling of a bird; the fairy mistress as in "Sir Launfal"; and the nature of the hero's antagonist, a Saracen giant who serves as guardian of the fairy.[1] We know this giant is a Saracen, as are many in romance, because of his "eastern" name, Olifaunt (line 808, cp. "elephant"),[2] and from the god he swears by, Termagaunt (line 810).[3] He is a perfect elephantine opponent for small Sir Thopas, and in stanza 18 Chaucer overturns the biblical story of David and Goliath[4] by giving the giant the slingshot and having the boy run away,[5] whereas the warrior's code in chivalric romance requires that a hero stand fast. Fytt II (i.e., the second part) offers an elaborate arming scene that echoes similar scenes in "Guy of Warwick" in its attention to individual items of dress—but during the proceedings Thopas gets comfort food, gingerbread snacks (854–56). In *The Canterbury Tales*, the previous religious "miracle" tale (line 691) told by the Pilgrim Prioress is in high

---

[1] The standard book currently on medieval giants is Jeffrey Jerome Cohen's *Of Giants: Sex, Monsters, and the Middle Ages* (Minneapolis: U of Minnesota P, 1999). In her earlier work, *The Matter of Araby in Medieval England* (New Haven: Yale, 1977), Dorothee Metlitzki has an entire chapter titled "The Saracen Giant."

[2] Among the Saracen or at least dark-skinned giants in English romance are Vernagu in "Rouland and Vernagu," "Astragot of Ethiop" in the "Sowdone of Babylone" (and his giantess wife Barrok), Ascopart in "Bevis of Hamtoun," Amoraunt and Colbrond in "Guy of Warwick," Gulfagor in "Ferumbras," and the list goes on. Gawain's antagonist in *Sir Gawain and the Green Knight*, though an enchanted Sir Bercilak, is allied to these giants by being notably "colored."

[3] The Saracen deity Termagaunt is also mentioned in "Guy of Warwick" and "Lybeaus Deconnus," both romances named at lines 898–900 of "Sir Thopas." Chaucer enjoys having his characters identify themselves with a place by swearing by a local religious figure, so by having the giant Olifaunt swear thus, he is parodying his own practice. Among many of the characters in *The Canterbury Tales* who swear by local saints and relics are the Oxford carpenter John in "The Miller's Tale" who swears by the Oxford "Seint Frydeswyde" (Frideswide; I 3449), the wife native to Trumpington in "The Reeve's Tale" who swears by the nearby "hooly croys of Bromeholm" (I 4286), and the two students from "fer in the north" (I 4015) in the same tale who suitably swear by the northern "Seint Cutberd" (Cuthbert; I 4127). Chaucer continues this practice throughout the tales as opportunity offers.

[4] Perhaps here Chaucer is inspired by the Goliath-like Saracen giant Vernagu, who is, according to Metlitzki, "explicitly derived from Goliath in the pseudo-Turpin chronicle of Charlemagne, the source of the Middle English (early fourteenth-century) 'Rouland and Vernagu' by way of a French version" (193). Chaucer could have known this romance because it is in the same Auchinleck manuscript as two of the romances he lists at the end of "Sir Thopas"; Chaucer may have been familiar with that or a similar collection. The illustrator of Thopas and Olifaunt in Sarah Teale's *Giants* (New York: Abrams, 1979), 126–27, captures some of what Chaucer says but not all: Olifaunt is represented as a large, fat giant with a long nose and elephant-looking ears that are, when one looks twice, actually two extra heads (see lines 842–43); he is wielding a slingshot to cast a stone at Sir Thopas, grown up but unbearded, who is fleeing anxiously on horseback.

[5] For a great many identifications of the romance themes Chaucer is parodying, with illustrative extracts, see Laura Hubbard Loomis's chapter on "Sir Thopas" in *Sources and Analogues of the Canterbury Tales*, ed. W.F. Bryan and Germaine Dempster (New York: Humanities Press, 1958), 486–559.

contrast to this one in terms of mood and genre, but it shares the teller's naiveté. Another possible relationship between the two stories is that the protagonist of her tale is a little boy, and, except for his exaggeratedly long yellow beard described at line 731, which could be a prop, Sir Thopas with his "sides small" (line 836, translated below as "slim") seems very much like a little boy dressing up and playing at being a knight.[6]

Chaucer amuses himself additionally with the structure of the three fytts or parts of "Sir Thopas," making each part half the length of the part preceding it.[7] The contrast between the longer lines of the bracketing conversations and the choppy meter of the tale itself is quite remarkable to the ear,[8] with the familiar iambic pentameter sounding almost like prose in contrast with the "cute" meter of the story. The tale should be read as one reads the verse tales of Dr. Seuss, with delight in the silliness of it.

---

[6] Lee Patterson examines this possibility in *Temporal Circumstances: Form and History in the Canterbury Tales* (New York: Palgrave Macmillan, 2006), 103–04, and concludes by describing "Sir Thopas" as "a charming representation of a child at play" (104). Cohen sees him instead as a doll throughout Chapter Four in *Of Giants*. Puppetry also comes to mind: scenes such as the confrontation between the little knight and the elephantish giant would work very well in a puppet show—though surely the knight should win. (The otherwise curious line 775 could well refer to a puppetry or hand-puppet horse.)

[7] For elaboration of this and related observations concerning size, see Cohen, "The Giant of Self-Figuration: Diminishing Masculinity in Chaucer's 'Tale of Sir Thopas,'" Chapter Four in *Of Giants*.

[8] The "Words of the Host to Chaucer" before the tale continues the elaborate seven-line stanza pattern of the preceding "Prioress's Tale," a stanza invented by Chaucer and used mainly for elevated subjects.

Sir Thopas

The Prologue to Sir Topaz
Behold the merry words of the Host to Chaucer

691 When all this miracle[9] was told, each man
So sober was, it wondrous was to see,
Until our Host began to joke again,
And for the first time looking down at me,[10]
695 He asked, "What man are you?" And then said he,
"You look as though you want to find a hare,
For always at the ground I see you stare.

"Approach now near and look up merrily.
Make way now, sirs; let this man have a place!
700 As well-shaped[11] in the waist as I, he'd be
An armful of a poppet[12] to embrace
For any woman slim and fair of face,
Appearing elvish in his concentration,
Engaging in no social conversation.[13]

705 "Say something now, and do it speedily.
Tell us a tale as other folk have done."
"Host," I replied, "don't be displeased with me,
For other tale truly I have none
Except a rhyme learned long ago for fun."
710 "Yes, good," he said. "Now from his look we'll hear
Some dainty thing, or so it would appear."

---

9   Miracle: "The Prioress's Tale."

10   Me: the pilgrim Chaucer, an imaginary person.

11   Well-shaped: stocky or plump.

12   Poppet: little doll (cp. puppet).

13   In "The General Prologue" to *The Canterbury Tales*, Chaucer the Pilgrim claims to have
spoken with all the other pilgrims: "So hadde I spoken with hem everichon/That I was of
hir felaweshipe anon" (I 31–32).

Here beginneth Chaucer's Tale of Sir Thopas

THE FIRST FYTT

     Listen, lords, with good intent,
And I shall tell, with merriment,
     The tale of what became

715   Of a most handsome, elegant
Knight, in joust and tournament.
     Sir Thopas was his name.

Born he was in a far countree,
In Flanders, far beyond the sea,
720   At Popering,[14] in the place
His noble father ruled, and he
Lord was of that fair countree
     According to God's grace.

Sir Thopas was a gallant knight.
725   His face, like the finest bread, was white;
     Each cheek was like a rose.
His lips were ruby-red and bright,
And this I tell you: he had quite
     A nice, attractive nose.

730   Saffron-yellow was his hair.
His yard-long beard was just as fair.
     His shoes were cordewain,[15]
His Brussels hose brown as a bear,
His silken robe a fine affair
735   That cost him many a jane.[16]

He liked to hunt the wild deer
And ride at hawking far and near,

---

[14] Poperinge is a town near the west coast of Belgium (Flanders) that Chaucer, as customs controller (from 1374 to 1386), would have known because of its importance in the cloth trade. He may have chosen this placename for its sound-association with "poppet," but it is interesting to observe that the town's traditional puppet-like character, "Squire Ghybe," carried in parades, is a parody of a knight and that the town "ambassador" is a giant having Saracen attributes. (Information from <http://www.poperinge.be/UK/index.htm>.)

[15] Cordewain: Spanish leather from Cordova in Spain.

[16] Jane: a coin of Genoa.

A goshawk on his wrist.
At archery he knew no fear;
740   At wrestling no one was his peer.
The prize he never missed.

Many a maiden in her bower
Longed for him with all her power,
     When she might better sleep.
745   Thopas was chaste, no idle lover,
And sweet as is the bramble flower
     Bearing the scarlet hip.

And so it happened then one day
(It's true, what I'm about to say),
750   He thought he'd take a ride,
And mounted on his dapple gray,
Bearing in hand his launcegay,[17]
     A long-sword by his side.

He galloped hard and never ceased
755   Through forests thick with many a beast,
     Yes!, both buck and hare;
And as he spurred to north and east,
I tell you, trouble not the least
     Almost befell him there.

760   Sweet grasses grew there, short and tall,
Licorice plants and cetewall,[18]
     Clove-gillyflower in rows,
And nutmeg, good for spicing ale
Whether it be new or "stale,"[19]
765   Or else for scenting clothes.

And birds sang there, it's true to say.
The sparrowhawk and popinjay[20]
     Were such a joy to hear!
The thrush sang also his sweet lay.

---

[17] Launcegay: a small lance, spear.

[18] Cetewall: a type of zedoary plant, a spice.

[19] Stale: aged by intent, like good wine.

[20] Popinjay: parrot. Observe that these are not song birds!

770 The turtledove upon her spray
    Was singing loud and clear.

  When Thopas heard the throstle[21] sing,
  He fell in love like anything,
    And spurred as if gone mad.
775 His steed so sweated that one might wring
  Him out from all that galloping,
    And bloody flanks he had.

  Then Thopas grew so very tired[22]
  From galloping across the sward
780   (So hearty was his zeal),
  That he lay down on that green sward,
  To rest his horse from working hard
    And let him have a meal.

  "Saint Mary, benedicite,"
785 He said. "What made Love[23] mad at me
    That he should bind me tight?
  All night a dream has promised me
  An elf-queen shall my lover be,
    To share my bed at night.

790 "To love an elf-queen I am sworn;
  For there's no mortal woman born
    Worthy to be my mate,
      In town.[24]
  All other women I forsake,
795 And as my love an elf-queen take,
    By dale and by down!

  He grabbed his saddle, climbed upon
  His horse, and sped o'er stile and stone,
    And all that country scanned

---

[21] Throstle: thrush (cp. line 769).

[22] Tired: this word must be pronounced in the American way (tard) for the rhyme with "sward" (turf).

[23] Love, i.e., the god of love, Cupid.

[24] Here Chaucer begins the "bob-and-wheel" stanza form familiar from *Sir Gawain and the Green Knight*.

800　For elf-queens, until he had gone
　　So far that he the secret won
　　　　To get to Fairyland
　　　　　　　　So wild;
　　For in that country was no one
805　Who dared to ride to him or run,
　　　　No woman and no child ...

　　Until there came a giant gaunt
　　Who called himself Sir Olifaunt,
　　　　A man of perilous deed.
810　He said, "Young knight, by Termagaunt,
　　Unless you leave these parts I haunt,
　　　　I soon shall slay your steed
　　　　　　　　With mace,[25]
　　For know, the Queen of Fairyland,
815　With her harper-and-drummer band,
　　　　Is dwelling in this place."

　　Sir Thopas said, "Then it must be:
　　Tomorrow I shall meet with thee
　　　　When I've my armor on.
820　I hope that then my launcegay
　　Will make thee sorrowfully pay
　　　　For what thou hast begun.
　　　　　　　　I fain[26]
　　Would pierce thy belly, if I may,
825　Before it is full prime[27] of day,
　　　　And here thou shalt be slain!"

　　Sir Thopas quickly then withdrew
　　While stones at him the giant threw
　　　　Out of a nasty sling.
830　But he escaped, our gallant knight,
　　Entirely by God's grace and might—
　　　　And his prompt exiting.

---

[25]　Mace: a type of club.

[26]　Fain: would like to.

[27]　Full prime: around 9 a.m..

THE SECOND FYTT

But listen, lords, now to my tale,
Merrier than the nightingale,
835   For more to you I'll roun[28]
Of how Sir Thopas, slim and hale,
Galloping over hill and dale,
      Went back again to town.

His merry men commanded he
840   To give him games and minstrelsy,
      For now it was his duty
To fight a giant who boasted three
Huge heads! He'd fight for jollity
      And for a lady's beauty.

845   "Come now," he said, "my minstrels all
And story-tellers who can recall
      Old tales for while I'm arming,
Romances of a royal hall,
Tales of pope and cardinal,
850   And lovers true and charming."

They fetched him first the sweet red wine,
And also mead in a mazeline,[29]
      And pastry made with spice,
Gingerbread so sweet and fine,
855   The licorice and cumin kind
      With sugar, that's so nice!

Next to his skin must Thopas don
His linen clothes,[30] then he put on
      His breeches and a shirt,
860   And over his shirt an aketon,[31]
And then a bright haubergeon
      Meant to protect his heart,

---

[28] Roun (a romance word): say.

[29] Mead in a mazeline: honey wine in a wooden bowl.

[30] Linen clothes: underwear.

[31] Aketon: quilted jacket that goes under the haubergeon or chainmail tunic.

And over that a hauberk[32] too,
The finest work made by a Jew,[33]
865   Plate-armor strong and bright,
And over that his cote-armor[34]
As white as is the pretty fleur-
De-lis.[35] In this he'd fight.

His shield was colored gold and red
870   With thereupon a wild-boar's head
Beside a ruby gay,
And there he swore on ale and bread
The mighty giant would soon be dead,
Come whatever may!

875   His jambeaux were of quirbolly,[36]
His sword's sheath made of ivory,
His helmet brassy-bright.
His saddle was of walrus bone,
His bridle shining like the sun,
880   Or maybe like moonlight.[37]

Of splendid cypress was his spear,
Not boding peace, but war and fear;
The head was sharply ground.
His destrier[38] was of dappled gray,
885   And it went ambling on its way,
Chubbily, around
The land ...
Look, my lords, we have a fit!
If you want any more of it,
890   I'm here at your command.

---

32 Hauberk: breastplate.
33 Made by a Jew: the Jews, like the Saracens, were famous for their fine metalwork.
34 Cote-armor: heraldic surcoat, a sort of open tunic bearing the knight's identifying coat of arms.
35 Fleur-de-lis (French): lily flower.
36 Jambeaux were of quirbolly: leg-armor of waxed leather.
37 Compare the description of the fairy lady's horse-trappings in "Thomas of Erceldoune."
38 Destrier: warhorse. Note that a fat warhorse (line 886) is an oxymoron.

THE THIRD FYTT

For goodness' sakes now, hold your tongue,
Both gallant knight and lady young,
    And hearken to my tale,
And I of fights and chivalry
895   And service to a fair lady
    Shall tell you without fail.

They speak of these romances high
Of Ypotis and good Sir Guy,
    Of Bevis and King Horn,
900   Sir Pleyndamour and Sir Libeaus,[39]
But Thopas takes the prize from those:
    For chivalry he was born!

His gallant steed he now bestrides
And forth upon his way he glides
905   As spark flies from the brand.
Upon his crest he bears a tower
In which is stuck a lily flower.
    God keep him in His hand!

Because he was adventurous,
910   He would not sleep in any house
    But lay down in his hood,[40]
His helmet pillowing his head.
Beside him, his fine destrier fed
    On grasses sweet and good.

915   Thopas himself drank from a well
As did the good Sir Percyvell,[41]
    So worthy was that knight—
Until one day ...[42]

---

[39] Libeaus: pronounce Li-BOWS. All except Pleyndamour (unknown) are famous heroes of romance.

[40] In his hood: i.e., ready for action.

[41] Percyvell: Sir Percival of the Round Table, hero of the medieval romance "Sir Percyvell of Gales."

[42] Anyone attentive to the rhyme scheme here should be able to complete this line with a standard story-telling cliché, like "it so befell ..." Chaucer is teasing the reader to do just that.

The Host's Words to the Pilgrim Chaucer

"No more of this! For God's sake let it be,"
920   Broke in our Host, "because you're making me
So tired of your confounded ignorance
That now, by God, you'd better stop at once!
My ears are aching from a speech so drasty.[43]
The devil take such rhyme; it's really nasty!
925   This may well be pure doggerel,"[44] said he.
"Why so?" said I. "Why will you not let me
Tell all my tale like any other man,
Since here I've rhymed the very best I can?"
"By God," our Host said, "plainly, in a word,
930   Your drasty rhyming isn't worth a turd!
You're doing nothing here but waste our time.
Sir, in a word, you shall no longer rhyme!"

[After further interchange with the Host of the Canterbury Pilgrimage, the pilgrim Chaucer will proceed to tell a more worthy and moral story, the "Tale of Melibee"—in prose.]

---

[43] Drasty: disgusting (literally, "crappy").

[44] Doggerel: banal rhyme. This is the first recorded appearance in English of this now-standard term for cliché-ridden verse.

CHAPTER 7

Emaré

P reserved in only a single manuscript of the early fifteenth century, "Emaré" is one of numerous European romances sharing the plot of an innocent woman being set adrift. These romances are usually identified either as belonging to a "Constance-Saga" cycle,[1] seeing the woman as patient victim, or a "Calumniated Queen" series, emphasizing the lies told about her.[2] Since the woman is usually of royal blood and is set adrift twice or more for different reasons, and the earliest stories do not include calumny, I have argued elsewhere that these stories might better be

---

[1] Named by A.B. Gough in his study "The Constance Saga," *Palaestra* 23 (1902): 1–84. The woman's name in this title comes from the two most famous versions of these romances in English, those told by Gower in Book II of his *Confessio Amantis* and by Chaucer (altering her name to Custance) in "The Man of Law's Tale." Edith Rickert took Gough's study farther in her two-part monograph, "The Old English Offa Saga," *Modern Philology* 2 (1904): 29–76; and 3 (1905): 321–76.

[2] Margaret Schlauch, *Chaucer's Constance and Accused Queens* (New York: Columbia UP, 1927). Since a lying accusation represents only one element of the plot, though a typifying one, the title seems inadequate.

called "Castaway Queen romances."[3] In the medieval Castaway Queen plot, the woman protagonist is set adrift (or, rarely, escapes to sea) as the result of family violence, often incest.[4] Though expected to die, she survives to come ashore in a foreign land, marries, may bear a child, and is set adrift once more when lies are told about her or the baby. Again she survives, manages to pull together her dispersed family, and finally returns home safely. This is a medieval elaboration of a very old story indeed, associated with the Mediterranean Sea and possibly with an ancient custom there, one that still prevails in places, of setting adrift an image of the local deity (these days the Virgin Mary), or perhaps more anciently a human sacrifice.[5]

The adventures of Emaré begin when her angry father has her cast away at sea for not accommodating his lustful desire, and her story follows the plot described above. Because the woman castaway is victimized, commentators remark upon her helplessness and compare her story to that of patiently suffering saints; and some of these maidens are indeed saintly in their patience. Chaucer's Custance in "The Man of Law's Tale" certainly is, and God comes to her aid when needed.[6] Others depend more on themselves. Florence of Rome, for example, defends her virtue with vigor, bashing out the teeth of a would-be rapist with a bed-warming stone, and several of these women learn to support themselves by means of their skills, as Florence does with herbal medicine and Emaré with her embroidery. Laskaya and Salisbury, whose edition has proven most helpful in revising this translation, place "Emaré" more firmly in the category of saintly sufferer than others might, observing that she, "as the long-suffering mother

---

[3] *Romancing the Goddess: Three Middle English Romances about Women* (Urbana: U of Illinois P, 1998), 3–7. For discussion of the calumny issue, see pp. 32–33. In the earliest version of the story in which the issue arises, the noblewoman, having drifted ashore in England, claims that lies were told against her, but analogues suggest that she has in fact performed the crimes for which she was cast away. Within the broader category of "Constance-Cycle" romances, the lady is not always royal and may be left to live or die in any wilderness location, not necessarily cast away at sea.

[4] Elizabeth Archibald situates this theme of the castaway woman's story within the broader context of medieval literature in her book *Incest and the Medieval Imagination* (Oxford: Clarendon Press, 2001).

[5] Walter Burkert, *Homo Necans: The Anthropology of Ancient Greek Sacrificial Ritual and Myths*, trans. Peter Bing (Berkeley: U of California P, 1983), 207; discussed in Osborn, *Romancing the Goddess*, 219–23.

[6] In another version of the story, the fairytale "Le Mannikin," the maiden's hands are cut off, which certainly emphasizes her helplessness! (For discussion of the theme of the victim's hands being severed or mutilated after incest or attempted incest, see Osborn, *Romancing the Goddess*, 213–18 and notes.). This "severed hands" feature suggests that the helpless maiden motif is not identical with the suffering saint motif, though they clearly can overlap, as in Chaucer's story.

of the next Holy Roman Emperor, is modeled after the Virgin."[7] But the holiness of neither mother nor son is emphasized in this story so much as is their calm resourcefulness. In sum, Custance seems saintly, Emaré more human: smart, devout,[8] surprisingly realistic (lines 625–36), sensibly cautious (not revealing her identity to strangers), manipulative though with grace, and patient in adversity but not specifically saintly about it. In fact, each of the "more human" women of these romances, in addition to being a more active agent than suggested by the "passive sufferer" designation, usually puts things right at the end of the story by her own efforts. Above all, each perseveres against astonishing odds, so that we may describe her as being not only the protagonist but also the heroine of her romance.

"Emaré" is, however, a Castaway Queen romance in the form of a Breton lay cast in English tail-rhyme stanzas, and thus it includes singsongy features that are pretty sure to puzzle or dismay the serious reader. Among these are the repetitive lines about Emaré's danger and hunger (lines 334–36, 682–84), and her tormenters, one after another, chanting "Alas, that I was made a man" and promptly fainting (lines 290–93, 556–57, 772–74). If one remembers that according to tradition the Breton lay was intended to be sung, these choral features may not be so disturbing.

Although "Emaré" follows the Castaway Queen plot to perfection, there is a magical aspect of the story that makes it different from all the others, the lady's glittering robe. Emaré's beauty alone provokes her father's ignoble desire, but then he has a robe made of the bejeweled length of cloth given to him by a friend, for her to wear at their proposed wedding, and he sets her adrift in it when she refuses him. The power of this robe is constantly emphasized, and though the quality of its magic is unclear, at least people in the story *think* it is magical or that Emaré wearing it is otherworldly.[9]

Two features of the robe are thematically important in the tale: it is extravagantly embroidered and set with jewels, and the artist who made it is a Saracen. The theme of women embroidering runs throughout the story, with Emaré exemplifying that skill, but she does not embroider magic into

---

[7] *The Middle English Breton Lays* (TEAMS Middle English Texts. Kalamazoo: Western Michigan UP, 2001), 183. It is rare that I disagree with Laskaya and Salisbury, whose introductions to the romances they edit in this volume I consider exemplary and even elegant, but in this case I think they overemphasize Emaré's "subjugation" and objectification in describing her as "an object exchanged" (149). She is not at all as passive as these terms imply.

[8] Emaré is devout, as the woman protagonist of a medieval story ought to be, and her devotion aids her, although we are also told that her suffering, sinless though it is, was ordained on high (lines 327, 675).

[9] See lines 244–45, 395–96, 446, and 700–02.

her work. The Saracen maker of the cloth does;[10] by embroidering four pairs of lovers into the four corners of her cloth she has created a love-token. Three pairs are famous lovers of romance: Ydóyne and Amadas,[11] Tristan and Isolde, and Florys and Blancheflour. The fourth pair is the Saracen noblewoman herself and the Sultan's son whom she desires. Despite the many other interpretations that have been proposed about the cloth's meaning, it seems clear that the maker intended it as the sort of charm that works through likeness. Thus when Emaré is wrapped in her robe, she is also implicated in the love stories of those four maidens, and her beauty is made magical by this Saracen artifact[12] that simultaneously endangers her at every point of her adventures. The magic of the robe is ambiguous rather than evil, because the viewer's attitude toward Emaré wearing it varies: some people perceive her as uncanny or an object of lust, and others simply admire her beauty. Perhaps it is safest to say that this gloriously bright robe "dazzles" its viewers, and when thus dazed they reveal much about themselves.

---

[10] This Saracen maiden is not represented as evil, as are Saracens in other Castaway Queen romances, and Saracens are presented as the enemy even in "Emaré," at line 483. As for the Sultan's mother in "The Man of Law's Tale," who takes murderous vengeance on all her Muslim subjects who have converted to Christianity and even kills her own son, one cannot reasonably read Chaucer's description of her mayhem with anything but horror, although recent attempts have been made to justify her actions.

[11] Gower mentions this romance in Book VI of his *Confessio Amantis*: Amans tells of his ear being fed with "redinge of romance / Of Ydoine and of Amadas, / That whilom weren in mi cas" (6.878–80). A translation by Ross G. Arthur of this Anglo-Norman romance is online at <http://www.yorku.ca/inpar/amadas_arthur.pdf>.

[12] It is a historical fact that the most amazingly intricate artifacts of the Middle Ages, often seeming magical to Western viewers, were made by craftsmen and scholars of the Middle East; witness the astrolabe.

Emaré

Oh, Jesus, king upon your throne,
Shaper of the sun and moon
   And all that gives delight,
Now grant us grace such deeds to do
5   That someday we may dwell with you
   In bliss called "heaven-light."
And you, his Mother, Heaven's queen,
Who's such a lovely go-between,
   Please bear our praying right
10   Up to your Son, so one day we
In Heaven above with Him may be—
   That Lord of greatest might.

Minstrels wandering far and wide,
Here and there on every side
15   In many a different land,
Wherever they begin to sing
Should mention first the Heavenly King
   Who made both sea and sand.
Now if you'll listen for a time,
20   I'll tell you a delightful rhyme
   (Though sad notes be among
The lighter ones) of a lady gay.
The lady's name was Emaré,
   And here I sing her song.

25   Her sire, an emperor of power,
Ruled from a castle and mighty tower.
   Sir Artyus[13] was he.
And he had other halls and bowers,
Fields and forests fair with flowers:
30   No greater lord could be.
The well-born lady that he wed
Was fair and lovely. Skin she had
   As white as ivory.

---

[13] This name is pronounced either AR-tyus or AR-tee-us, two syllables or three depending on the demands of the meter. The women's names Eranye, Emare and Egare (or Egarye) are all stressed on the first syllable and end, respectively, with the sounds "yay" and "ay."

They called that empress Eranye;
35   No lady with a more loving way
        Was ever known than she.

Sir Artyus was the best of men
In all the world who was living then,
        A strong and valorous knight.
40   Courtly he was in every way
Both to the young and the old and gray,
        And treated people right.
Just one child in all his life
Had he begotten of his wife,
45   And she was fair and bright.
Forsooth, her name again I'll say:
They called that baby Emaré.
        She was a lovely sight.

And when her mother gave her birth,
50   She was the fairest child on earth,
        Her mother's outcome, though,
Was sad, for she, so fair and good,
Had died before her baby could
        Walk or talk, and so
55   The father sent his pretty baby
Out to be fostered by a lady
        People called Abró.[14]
She taught her proper courtesy,
And, with some others, embroidery:
60   How maidens ought to sew.

Abró taught well that maiden small
How to comport herself in hall
        While she was yet in bower.
Courteous was small Emaré
65   Both to the young and the old and gray,
        And white as a lily flower,
And also skilled and quick of hand.
Everyone loved her in that land
        And wished to honor her.

---

[14] Apparently a name made up for the story: medieval Latin "abra" means "female servant."

70
Now let us leave the maiden there
With Dame Abró so good and fair
   And speak of the emperor.

This emperor of noble blood
Was a courteous lord, and good
75
   In every sort of way.
And later, when his wife was dead,
A quiet widower's life he led,
   Though much inclined to play.
So when the King of Sicily
80
Came to visit Artyus, he
   Was glad for him to stay.
A present the Sicilian brought,
A cloth that worthily was wrought
   In a country far away.

85
Upon his knee, the noble knight
Sir Tergaunt offered his lord the bright
   Roll of embroidery.
The cloth that he presented him
Was studded with many a precious gem,
90
   As thickly as could be:
Topazes, diamonds clear as ice,
And other stones of equal price
   Were beautiful to see.
Toadstones,[15] rubies, agates fair,
95
Exquisitely were set out there,
   I tell you truthfully.

They hung the cloth upon the wall,
But Artyus could not see at all
   The cloth he gazed upon.
100
The glare of many a precious gem
Into his eyes had blinded him.
   He said, "What's going on?"
And then he bellowed angrily,
"This is a fairy trick on me,

---

[15] *Crapowtes* in Middle English, these were precious stones thought to grow in a toad's head and to have various medicinal and semi-magical uses. For example, besides being an antidote for poison, *crawpowtes* might increase a man's sexual potency and his skill in battle.

105   Or some such phenomenon!"
The King of Sicily calmly spoke:
"Of treasures owned by Christian folk,
There's no comparison!"

The daughter of a heathen Emir
110   Designed this cloth, or so I hear,
And wrought it all with pride,
Portraying lovers and their ilk
In threads of gold and azure silk
With jewels on every side.
115   The story that we have in hand
Says precious stones from every land
Were sought for far and wide.
For seven winters it was sewn
Before she felt it could be shown—
120   'Twas not a thing to hide!

Embroidered in one corner was
Ydóyne[16] and Amadas,
Their love that was so true.
And they were shown, for honest love,
125   Entwined with a true-love flower of
Gems of a brilliant hue:
With sapphire and with carbuncle,
Chalcedony[17] and onyx, all
Set into gold brand-new,
130   And diamonds, rubies, many a stone;
And singing troubadors were shown,
With all their instruments, too.

The second corner showed the pair
Sir Tristan and Isolde the Fair,
135   Most elegant to see.
Because the love was right, between
The two of them, with gems the scene
Was thick as it might be.

---

[16]   Pronounce this name Ee-DOH-ee-nay, with four syllables.

[17]   Chalcedony, sometimes spelled Calcedony (Kassydonys in Middle English), is a type of
quartz having a somewhat waxy luster. Its lapidary magic was especially associated with
eloquence.

With rubies and with topazes
140   And other worthy stones, it was
    Agleam exquisitely,
And set with toadstones, agates fair,
And precious stones beyond compare,
    I tell you truthfully.

145   In the third corner were lovers more,
Floris and Lady Blancheflour,[18]
    Each to the other dear,
And they were shown, for honest love,
Entwined with a true-love flower of
150   Jewels most bright and clear.
Many a knight and senator there
Were also shown in emeralds rare
    And faultless; and there were
Diamonds, corals pink and white,
155   Crystals, yellow chrysolite,
    And garnets everywhere.

The final corner showed the son
Of the Sultan of Babylon,
    And with him, standing near,
160   Was she who loved like life itself
Him for whose sake she made the cloth,
    The daughter of the Emir.
Before this maid, a unicorn
Lifted his solitary horn
165   High into the air,
And birds and flowers on every side
Gleamed with gems found far and wide,
    And imagery everywhere.

And when the cloth at last was made
170   And to the sultan was conveyed,
    It was a lovely sight.
Sir Tergaunt said, "My father won
This cloth from the Sultan of Babylon
    With mastery and might.

---

[18] Here, the name Blancheflour has three syllables. Elsewhere, the meter may indicate only two syllables.

175 To show his love he gave to me
This cloth that I have especially
 Brought you, sir, rich and bright."
He gave it to the emperor
Who courteously thanked him for
180 The treasure, as was polite.

The King of Sicily stayed there
Enjoying life with the emperor
 As long as he could stay.
In due course he decided, though,
185 Politely that he had to go,
 And went upon his way.
And then the lonely emperor
Thought of his daughter, longing for
 A word with Emaré.
190 So by a messenger he conveyed
His wishes to that gentle maid,
 Bright as a summer's day.

His messengers made ready quickly,
Going with music through the city,
195 Passing through throng and press
By thoroughfare and alley way
Until they came to Emaré,
 So pretty in her dress.
She who raised her, Dame Abró,
200 Into the carriage stepped also,
 The maiden's governess.
And they went to Sir Artyus, who
Came out himself a mile or two;
 That meeting was of the best!

205 This maiden, white as a lily flower,
Stepped down to meet the emperor.
 Two knights were in the lead.
Her father, who with great renown
Bore on his head the kingdom's crown,
210 Dismounted from his steed.
When they were both upon their feet,
He hugged and kissed his daughter sweet

And they turned to proceed
In joy, the maiden with her father,
215   And to the palace they went together,
In story as we read.

Great lords had gathered there to eat.
They washed and sat down to their meat,
And quickly they were plied
220   With food and drink. The maiden fair
Was led up to her father's chair
And seated by his side.
The fairest woman of that day,
She smiled whenever he looked her way.
225   He often looked, and sighed.
Then with his daughter he fell in love
And gazed upon her, thinking of
Taking her for his bride!

When after dinner he'd withdrawn
230   And to his royal chamber gone,
He called his council there.
He said they must go on a mission
To get for him the Pope's permission
To wed. They did not dare
235   Question the emperor's intent,
And so away the messengers went
And earls went with them, where
Quickly from the court of Rome
They brought his dispensation home,
240   To wed his daughter fair.

And then the emperor was elated!
He ordered a wedding robe created
Out of that cloth of gold.
When in that shining robe the woman
245   Dressed, she seemed no longer human,
Cast in the common mold.
And then the emperor, turning to
His daughter proclaimed, "I'll marry you,
So lovely to behold."

250 That worthy maiden, in her gown,
  Said, "Nay, sir! God in Heaven would frown
   If we should be so bold.

  "If it befell that we were wed
  And played together in your bed,
255   Lost we both should be.
  The word would spread out far and wide
  Through all the world on every side,
   By rumor, endlessly.
  You are a lord with reputation,
260 So let God guide you. To your nation
   Don't bring such misery.
  That to the altar I should go
  With my own father, I say no,
   I never will agree!"

265 The emperor, swelling up with wrath,
  Spoke in his rage a mighty oath
   That slain the maid should be.
  At once he ordered a noble boat
  Prepared for setting his child afloat
270   In that embroidery.
  No money must be in her purse,
  No food, no drink to slake her thirst,
   When cast upon the sea.
  Soon the lady was far from shore
275 Without an anchor or an oar,
   A heart-rending destiny!

  There came a wind, I understand,
  That blew the boat away from land
   And swept it out of sight,
280 And now to the emperor came the thought
  That possibly his deed had not
   Been absolutely right.
  He stood there thinking with a frown,
  Then fainted suddenly, falling down.
285   He was a sorry sight.

The noble lords who stood around
Caught up the emperor from the ground
   And comforted him all night.

When Artyus recovered, he
290   Cried out and said remorsefully,
     "Alas, my daughter dear!
Alas that I was made a man!
Oh, wretched lecher that I am!"
   He shed then many a tear.
295   "Against God's law I sought to do
Harm to my daughter, in faith so true,
   And now she is not here!"
The tears then poured out from his eyes,
And all his lords heaved mighty sighs
300   And also shed a tear.

Then neither young nor old could keep
From crying, nor could they cease to weep
   For her of the golden hair.
So in their ships they quickly went
305   Out searching for the innocent
     Maiden, so young and fair.
Though over all the seas they sought her,
They could not find the emperor's daughter,
   And soon they came back where
310   The emperor waited. Now let us leave
Him there, and of her on the wave
   I shall now declare.

The lady floated forth alone,
To God in Heaven making moan,
315   And to His Mother too.
Far she was driven by wind and rain
And mighty storms on the bounding main
   That hard against her blew.
I have heard minstrels sing the tale,
320   How, far from home and land, her sail
     Over the ocean flew.

Driven terrified deep to deep,
She hid her head and began to weep,
    For nothing could she do.

325 Now Emaré was in this plight
A little over a seven-night,
    According to God's will.
With heart full of care and sighing sore,
She knew her sorrow ordained of yore,
330   So ever she lay still.
At last she was driven onto land
Through the grace of God's own hand
    That all things may fulfil.
After days of constant danger
335 She was nearly mad with hunger.
    Woe to the winds of ill![19]

Her ship was driven onto a land
Called Galys (Wales, I understand).
    That was a pleasant shore.
340 The king's own steward dwelt nearby
Within a castle proud and high.
    His name was Sir Kadore.
Each day he strolled upon the sand,
And with him anyone at hand,
345   A squire or two, or more.
On this fair morning he went out
With two good knights and strolled about,
    When suddenly, before ...

Their very eyes at the surf's edge loomed
350 A boat, and something in it gleamed.
    They thought it must be fey.[20]
The three went toward it nonetheless
And found the lady in her dress
    Where in the boat she lay.
355 So long without any food she'd been,
It made them ache, she was so thin,
    About to pass away.

---

[19] Winds of ill: bad luck.

[20] Fey: fairy, magical.

Kadore politely asked her name.
She changed it to almost the same,
    And called herself Egaré.[21]

360

Then much concerned for her, Kadore
Led homeward from that wild shore
    The lady from the sea.[22]
She'd had no food when under sail,
And thin, it seemed now, as a rail
    Under her dress was she.
Now to his castle they came apace.
They took her to a quiet place
    And fed her copiously
With every delicate kind of food
They thought might do her any good,
    That in that place might be.

365

370

When slowly Emaré the fair
With meat and drink was able there
    Her color to regain,
She taught the women how to sew
Embroidered hangings that would glow
    With silks from shining skein.[23]
Courtly she was in every way
Both to the young and old and gray,
    Adored by great and plain,
And able to sew up anything
To clothe an emperor or king,
    Or baron, earl, or swain.

375

380

Kadore then had an inspiration.
He planned a happy celebration
    For his lord the king.
Many musicians he had come
To play on psaltry, horn and drum,
    Others on wind and string.

385

390

---

[21]   Egaré: (French) means outcast.

[22]   "From the sea" is one possible meaning of her real name, in Latin: *e-mare*.

[23]   A "skein" (the word introduced here for the rhyme) is a coil of thread. The young women embroidering hangings, no doubt including banners, would be working with skeins of silken thread.

The lady, regal now and slim,
Alone in the hall was serving them
    Before that noble king.
She wore the robe that shone so bright
395   It seemed like an unearthly light,
    And she no earthly thing.

The king of Wales, who gazed upon
The lady, had encountered none
    So fair that she could hold
400   His heart, and he was with the sight
So dazzled he could not eat a bite,
    But wished only to behold.
She was so courtly in her manner,
The king's love firmly settled on her,
405   In story as it is told.
So when that dinnertime was through,
He went to his chamber, calling to
    All of his barons bold.

He called for Sir Kadore to come
410   With other barons to his room.
    They waited there until
His dukes and nobles, wise of lore,
Were all assembled there before
    Their king, then asked his will.
415   The King of Wales in rich array
To Sir Kadore had this to say.
    His words were amiable:
"Good sir, whence comes that lovely maid
Who served me, graciously arrayed?
420   Please tell me, if you will."

Then said Kadore, I understand,
"She's an earl's daughter from a land
    That I have never seen.
I sent for her to come to me
425   To teach my children courtesy,[24]
    And up in their rooms she's been.

---

[24] Courtesy: i.e., the manners of court.

The needlework by her white hands
Is quite the best in Christian lands
 Of any I have seen."
430 Then said that powerful ruler there,
"I wish to have that maiden fair.
 I'll wed her as my queen."

The noble king, with this intent,
After his royal mother sent
435 To hear what she would say.
They also brought the lovely maid,
Fair Egaré, so well arrayed,
 Agleam like a summer's day.
The cloth upon her shone so bright
440 When she was in it, like a light
 On gentle Egaré,
That said the old queen, with a laugh,
"I never saw a woman half
 So glittering and so gay."

445 And then she said these words unkind:
"My son, that robe! This is a fiend
 Whom you have thought to wed.
So if you want your mother's blessing,
You must not ever have this wedding!
450 Nay, God forbid!" she said.
Then said that powerful ruler, "Mother,
I will have that maid, however!"
 When by the hand he led
The maid, then said the angry queen,
455 Turning for home, "I do not mean
 To stay to see you wed."

And so he married his lady fair,
And great were the efforts to prepare,
 Appropriately, the hall.
460 The noble lords were served all night:
Duke and baron, earl and knight,
 Persons both great and small.
So many came to that abode,
The castle nearly overflowed—

465   This does the tale recall.
      And there was every kind of thing
      Right for the wedding of a king,
         And minstrels played for all.

      When the wedding feast was done
470   And lords were leaving one by one,
         A seemly sight to see,
      The king was left there with his queen.
      As great the love there was between
         The two as there could be.
475   She was so sweet and courteous,
      I've never heard of a lady who was
         More loving than was she.
      Quite soon that lady meek and mild
      Conceived, and she grew big with child,
480   As God willed, healthily.

      The King of France, around that time,
      Was under duress. Attacking him
         Was many a Saracen.
      So sending a message to his friend,
485   He asked for him and others to lend
         A hand; his need was keen.
      The King of Wales prepared for war,
      Gathering warriors near and far
         In armor bright and clean.
490   Then said the king to Sir Kadore
      And other lords who stood before
         His throne, "Care for my queen!"

      The King of France called everyone,
      His under-kings and, sparing none,
495   His knights and clerics too.
      Only the steward was left at home
      To serve the fair queen pale as foam,
         For nothing of war he knew.
      As long as God's will let it be,
500   Beneath her smock quite prettily

The baby lay and grew,
Until at last she bore a lad.
A double royal mark he had,[25]
    As king's sons often do.

505 When the time for christening came,
Upon that royal child the name
    Of Segramore was bestowed,
And Sir Kadore then wrote to tell
The king the news that all was well,
510   A duty that he owed.
He quickly wrote down many a word
And sent the letter to his lord,
    As proper. But behold:
The messenger whom he told to hurry
515 With the king's mother stopped to tarry
    When past her house he rode.

Receiving well that messenger,
She asked him to report to her
    What child the queen had had.
520 "Madam, she had a little boy,
A fair man-child and all her joy,
    And now she lies in bed."
She gave for the news he brought to her
Forty shillings and a cloak of fur,
525   So he was richly clad.
She filled his cup with ale and wine,
And when she saw that it was time,
    Upstairs she led the lad.

The moment he began to snore,
530 The queen came through his chamber door.
    Wicked was her desire!
She took the letter from his cloak
And up she sent it in the smoke
    That rose from his bedroom fire.

---

[25] The identifying birthmark of a royal child is an occasional romance motif. The most famous English example of this is Havelok's birthmark, described at line 604 of his romance. Young Segramore's *double* royal mark implies that both his parents were royal. Emaré has not revealed her status to the king.

535 And then she wrote an evil letter
  Saying the queen had borne a devil
   And no one dared come nigh her.
  Three heads he had, she wrote, of bear,
  Dragon and lion, and too much hair!
540   Thus was that queen a liar.

  In the morning, when it was day,
  The messenger went on his way
   By roads both low and high,
  Arriving in his cloak of fur
545 Where the king and his armies were,
   Bearing his lord a lie.
  The king took the letter in his hand
  And read it and, as I understand,
   A tear came to his eye.
550 As he was standing reading it,
  Down he fell in a fainting fit,
   So sad he thought he'd die.

  But noble lords who stood around
  Soon caught the king up from the ground.
555   His heart was full of woe.
  Sorely he wept and said, "Alas,
  That ever born a man I was,
   That ever it should be so!
  Alas that I was made a king
560 And then must wed the fairest thing
   That ever on earth did go!
  Alas that Jesus chose to send
  A child as loathsome as a fiend
   To come between us so!"

565 But seeing that grief made nothing better,
  He sighed and wrote another letter,
   Sealing it with his seal.
  This was the message of the king:
  That they should help her in everything
570   Until she could fully heal.
  And everyone should do their best
  To carry out her least request

Both in woe and weal.
The messenger took it from his hand
575 And rode by the same route through the land,
And stopped to take a meal

With the old queen, and stayed all night.
Received so well and treated right,
He let the old queen ply
580 Him with the wine that stole his reason,
But never did he think of treason
As that long night went by.
When he was deep into his dreams,
The wicked queen began her schemes.
585 She sought until her eye
Lit on that letter, then wrote another
Ordering that the fair young mother
Be cast on the sea to die.[26]

She must be led down to the shore
590 Clad in the gleaming robe she wore;
With her, her child should be.
No money should be in her purse,
No food, no drink to slake her thirst,
When cast upon the sea.
595 "On penalty of your family's health
And the free life you lead yourself,
You must ignore each plea."
The messenger, who knew no guile,
Went riding home for many a mile
600 Through wilderness, wearily.

And when that messenger came home,
The steward, taking the letter from
His hand, began to read.
Sorely he sighed and said, "Alas,
605 A dreadful thing has come to pass!
This is a doleful deed."

---

[26] Casting an unwanted person away at sea was the "clean" form of execution, relieving the
perpetrator of guilt, since if God wanted to save someone adrift at sea He easily could do
so. Old Irish law actually includes explicit rules for the distance from shore to which the
castaway should be towed out and abandoned.

And as he stood there reading it,
He suddenly fell in a fainting fit;
 His heart began to bleed.
610 And there was no one, old or young,
Who did not weep at what was done
 To the lady in her need.

That lady, hearing in the hall,
The lamentation, went to call
615 The steward: "What can be
The trouble here? What's gone amiss?
Tell me exactly what it is.
 Hold nothing back from me."
Then mournfully the steward said,
620 "This is the letter I just read
 That caused such woe to me."
She took the letter from his hand
And read therein the cruel command
 To cast her to the sea.

625 But then, "Be calm, good sir," said she.
"You do not have to mourn for me,
 And you must not ignore,
To your own peril, the king's command
Here in this letter in my hand,
630 That there's some reason for.
Perhaps he thinks he wedded poorly,
Marrying me, a simple lady,
 And now feels shame therefore.
So greet my lord and say from me
635 That nobler born there could not be
 A babe any lady bore."

Much was the sorrow, much the woe,
When Emaré to the ship must go.
 They wept and wrung their hands.
640 The lady, walking meek and mild,
Bore in her arms the little child
 And took her leave of land.
When she went floating out to sea
In that bright robe, so gleamingly,

645   Grown men swooned on the sand.
         Sorely they wept and said, "Alas,
         That such an evil should come to pass!
             Woe to this command!"

         The lady and the little child
650   Floated away on the waters wild.
             Her luck was not the best.
         Across her face the collar wide
         Of that bright robe she pulled to hide
             The churning ocean, lest
655   Of those great billows she'd be afraid.
         Then down upon a plank she laid
             Herself, and to her breast
         She clutched the child, while from below
         Great waves were smiting blow on blow
660   With many an awful blast.

         And when the child began to weep,
         She sang him sadly back to sleep,
             His mouth upon her breast.
         "If only past these waves that roar
665   So high," she said, "I could get to shore,
             Whether to east or west,
         Then well ought I to curse thee, sea,
         When I am guiltless, for beating me."
             Sorely she was distressed.
670   But then she sat up, saying a prayer
         To Jesus and his Mother dear,
             The way that she knew best.

         Now was the lady in this plight
         A little over a seven-night,
675   According to God's will.
         With heart full of care and sighing sore,
         She knew her sorrow ordained of yore,
             So ever she lay still.
         At last the waves drove her to Rome
680   Through grace of God on Heaven's throne
             Who all things may fulfil.
         After days of constant danger,

She was nearly mad with hunger.
　　Woe to luck gone ill!

685　There in that capital city, Rome,
A wealthy merchant made his home,
　　Jordan by name, and he
Had plenty of wealth in gold and treasure.
He often liked to take his pleasure
690　　In walking by the sea,
When he went out on this occasion,
Taking a walk beside the ocean
　　And wishing alone to be,
He found a boat cast up on shore
695　And in it a lady weeping sore,
　　For woebegone was she.

The robe upon her shone so bright
That he was started by the light
　　Her glistening garment shed,
700　And in his heart he was afraid
That she was not an earthly maid,
　　But something else instead.
Yet, "What's your name," he asked her, "pray?"
And "Lord," she said, "I'm Egaré,
705　　Lying here in dread."
Then up he took her, and that fair
Lady with her baby there
　　Homeward the merchant led.

He brought her to his house in Rome
710　And welcomed kindly to his home
　　That lady fair and bright.
He asked his wife to bring some food,
Meat and drink, whatever was good,
　　And feed that lady right.
715　"Whatever it is that she may crave,
Whatever she desires to have,
　　Give it to her tonight,
For she so long has had to live
Deprived of food that you must give
720　　Her comfort with all your might."

And now the lady stayed with them,
And any food for which her whim
   Prompted, she had at will.
Courtly she was in every way
725 Both to the young and old and gray,
   To lowly and notable.
Her son began to grow and thrive,
And soon was the prettiest child alive,
   Fair as a flower on hill.
730 She sewed bright silken tapestries
And taught her small son courtesies,
   But ever was mournful still.

When Segramore was seven years old
And growing up both wise and bold,
735   Well formed of flesh and bone,
His clothing showed his mother's pride,
And well could he mount a horse and ride;
   More courtly child was none.
Young Segramore was loved by all,
740 Both in the bower and in the hall
   In company or alone.
Now let us leave them there in Rome
And speak of the king returning home,
   His siege and battle done.

745 As soon as the siege was broken, he
Set out for Wales victoriously,
   With great delight and pride.
His dukes and earls of rich estate,
Barons and knights both noble and great,
750   Came riding by his side,
And Sir Kadore, his steward, then
Rode up to him with many men
   As fast as he could ride.
Of all that happened, everything
755 In hall or bower, he told the king,
   Events both far and wide.

The king interrupted, "In God's name,
Good Sir Kadore, you're much to blame

For what you've chosen first
760   To tell me. What you ought to say
Is news of my lady Egaré,
    Her whom I love the most!"
The steward's heart then nearly broke.
He said, "My lord, is this a joke?
765   Of kings are you not the best?
Look at the letter you sent to me.
As you yourself may clearly see,
    I carried out your behest."

The king took up that letter to read,
770   And when he saw the wicked deed,
    He went all pale and wan.
Sorely he wept and cried, "Alas,
That ever conceived and born I was,
    Or ever made a man!
775   Good Sir Kadore, I swear to thee
This letter was never written by me
    Or sealed by my own hand."
Then both men wept and thought it ill.
"Alas," said the king, "if it's God's will…!"
780   And they fainted on the sand.

The great lords who around them stood
Caught up their king and then the good
    Kadore, with sympathy.
When both came to, the weeping king
785   Showed him the letter numbering
    The baby's heads as three.
"Ah, lord," Kadore said, "This I swear,
I never said that anywhere.
    Alas, how may this be?"
790   Then for the messenger they sent.
The king asked him which way he went
    To make delivery.

"Right past your mother's house," said he.
"Alas," said the king, "how could there be
795   A mother so unkind?
For treason she shall be burnt, for I

Give this judgment: that she must die,
　　And that is my command!"
The great lords modified between
800　Themselves this judgment on the queen
　　Who wickedly purloined
The letters. They sent her from the nation,
Seizing all her accumulation
　　Of castle, tower and land.

805　When she had fled across the foam,
The King of Wales remained at home,
　　And heavy was his air.
Heart full of sorrow, sighing sore,
Many a moan he uttered for
810　　His Egaré the fair.
And seeing any child at play,
He wept and said then, "Wellaway,
　　My little son so dear!"
So sad he was that no one could
815　Cheer up that king who was so good,
　　Until the seventh year.

The thought came to him there at home
Of how his lady white as foam
　　Had drowned to save his soul.
820　"Through grace of God who is our hope,
I'll go to Rome to see the pope
　　With penance as my goal!"
He ordered ships then, filling them
With worldly treasures to the brim,
825　　Good presents to cajole
His men, and many alms he gave,
Hoping thereby his soul to save
　　To make his spirit whole.

The sailors, worthy men at sea,
830　Dressing their tackle expertly
　　In an experienced way,
Drew up the sail and laid out oar,
Blessing their luck for the weather, for
　　The wind blew right, that day.

835   They sailed over the salty foam
       By grace of God on Heaven's throne
          Who holds over all His sway,
       And in the city when they came
       They lodged in a burgess's house, the same
840   Wherein lodged Emaré.

       Observing this, she called her son
       To come at once, for now begun
          Was his important test.
       She said, "My darling son, today,
845   Please do exactly as I say,
          And for it you'll be blessed.
       The very finest clothes you shall
       Wear to serve the king in the hall;
          Richly you'll be dressed.
850   And look, son: serve so courteously
       That there is no way you could be
          Challenged for being best.

       "When serving the after-dinner sweet,
       Kneel down quickly at his feet
855   And take his hand in thine.
       After this take his goblet up
       And pour into that golden cup
          A draught of honey-wine.
       And what he then shall say to you,
860   Come back at once and tell me, to
          Gain God's blessing and mine!"
       The child then went into the hall
       Where gathered were those rich lords all
          Clad in their garments fine.

865   Those noble lords both great and good
       Washed and waited for plates of food,
          Each borne by a troubadour.
       And then the child so courteously served
       That everybody who observed
870   Loved and praised him for
       His manners. Those who looked upon
       The child, said never had they seen one

Who plates more gracefully bore.
The king then asked him, just for fun,
875 "What is your name, my little son?"
He answered, "Segramore."

The King of Wales gave such a sigh
And was so sad he thought he'd die,
For *his* son was called so.
880 Truly I say (I tell no lies)
The tears came pouring from his eyes,
So heartfelt was his woe.
But quietly he began to eat,
While looking upon the child so sweet.
885 He loved him greatly, though.
Therefore he asked the burgess later,
"Is this your son? Are you the father?"
And he replied, "That's so."

The noble lords all, after they ate,
890 Washed their hands then, to await
The final delicacy.
The child whose manner so appealed
Brought in the king's dessert, and kneeled
And served him courteously.
895 The king then to the burgess said,
"Sir, let me have this little lad,
If thy will it should be.
I'll make him lord of town and tower,
Of many a mighty hall and bower.
900 I love him especially."

When he had served the king so well,
Segramore went to his mother to tell
Her all he could understand.
"My son, when he's about to go
905 (Your father, but this he does not know),
Go up and take his hand.
Bid him come speak to Emaré
Who changed her name to Egaré
In Wales, his own dear land."
910 The child again went to the hall

Among those great lords, one and all,
And served in the manner grand.

When they were well replete at last
After a final good repast
915   Of bread and ale and wine,
The king stood up and turned to go
Into his chamber. He met there, though,
The child who led him in
And said, "Sir, if your will it be,
920   Take my hand and come with me,
For I am of your kin!
Come and speak with Emaré
Who changed her name to Egaré,
Lady so fair of skin."

925   So sad the King of Wales became
On hearing the young boy speak the name
Of his beloved queen,
He said, "My son, why say you so?
Why thus upbraid me for my woe
930   And what should not have been?"
Nevertheless he went on down,
Then saw her coming in her gown,
The brightest ever seen.
He took her in his arms and they
935   Fainted together dead away,
For joy and love so keen.

Catching them up from the chamber floor,
Lord, how glad was Sir Kadore
At seeing the good king fold
940   His lady in his arms so tight!
Other lords also thought that sight
Delightful to behold.
And thus the queen they'd cast to sea,
Through grace of God in Trinity,
945   Recovered from cares so cold.
Let's leave her there and speak now further
Of Artyus, her royal father
Of whom this tale first told.

The emperor of whom we told
950 By now was getting rather old
   And thought about his sin,
Of how he ordered cast away
His lovely daughter Emaré
   At sea, so fair of skin.
955 He thought he'd go to see the Pope,
And ask for penance in the hope
   That Heaven he might win.
So he sent messengers from home
Who soon thereafter came to Rome
960   To find their lord an inn.

On seeing them, fair Emaré
Asked her husband, "Sir, please stay
   And meet this lord, for me.
And dearest sir, in everything
965 Acquaint yourself with this other king.
   An honor it will be."
The King of Wales said to his queen,
"In Christian lands there's never been
   A greater lord than he."
970 "And now," she said, "whatever betide,
To meet that great lord go to ride
   With a noble company."

She gave instructions to her son
About how everything should be done
975   And how he should behave:
"My son, you must show even more
Courtesy now to the emperor.
   Be gentle, somewhat grave,
And when he kisses your father, you
980 Must see if he will kiss you too.
   Then bow to him, and crave
That he come speak with Emaré,
The daughter that he cast away:
   Himself the order gave."

985 Now comes the emperor to Rome.
Now see the King of Wales come

And toward him proudly ride!
Now is the child a prince indeed,
Riding along on a noble steed
990   Beside his father with pride.
And now the emperor, when they meet,
Casts back his hood to kiss the sweet
    Child at the stranger's side.
And other lords now also kiss
995 The young boy Segramore, for this
    Affection they do not hide.

The emperor was admiring greatly
This child riding so close and stately,
    His face so young and fair.
1000 When Segramore held back his steed,
Of this the King of Wales took heed.
    The others who were there
Allowed him to speak to him alone:
"Sir, for the honor of your throne,
1005   My words you now must hear.
Come now to speak with Emaré
Who changed her name to Egaré
    And is your daughter dear."

The emperor then grew pale, and said,
1010 "Why thus upbraid me? She is dead.
    There's nothing to be done."
"Sir, if you will, I'll bring you where
The lady waits for you, so fair
    A face to look upon."
1015 And so the emperor went with him
And saw approach that lady slim,
    Walking all alone.
Then off his steed the emperor leapt,
And eagerly into his arms he swept
1020   Her whom he'd thought was gone.

Joyful was that reunion for
The king, the noble emperor,
    And also Emaré,
And likewise for Sir Segramore

1025　Who later was the emperor
　　　　And ruled well many a day.
　　　And great was the feast that they held the
　　　For all the loyal noblemen,
　　　　As those who tell this say.
1030　For this is one of the Breton lays
　　　They used to tell in the olden days;
　　　　It's called the "Plaint d'Garyé."[27]

　　　And so here ends the story.
　　　Jesus on Thy throne above,
1035　Grant us to live with thee in love
　　　In thy perpetual glory!
　　　　　　　　　Amen.

---

[27] "Plaint d'Garyé" (French): "Lament of the Outcast." No such romanc
It is common practice for an author to claim to be reworking a romanc
previously read; see line 216, for example.

CHAPTER 8

Sir Gowther

In the European tale of "Robert the Devil," the devil's son finds out about his unfortunate heritage and fights against it. "Sir Gowther" is an English version of that tale, composed around 1400 and presenting the reinterpreted story with interest and elegance. Although the romance has been described in terms of its religious aspect as "penitential," this designation, confirmed in particular by the ending, is nevertheless reductive because this brief story also invites exploration of numerous issues of special interest to twenty-first-century readers. These issues include identity politics, masculinities, women's agency, abjection, orientalism, animals and ethics, handicapped protagonists, and even a curious sort of "date rape," followed by the victim's need to suppress it (a well-known phenomenon). More traditionally recognized thematic elements include the shape-shifter, here a demon rather than a fairy, but these identities overlap; a magical greyhound; a lady watching from a tower, as in "Sir Launfal"; and innately evil Saracens. Although Sir Gowther is not an actual shape-shifter like his demon father, after his parentage has been revealed he goes through an extraordinary series of changes. First his nature develops from that of a wild beast to a tame one; then, as his socialization reaches a higher level, he passes through spiritual changes reflected in the armor he is given in response to prayer. Finally, two different kinds of muteness are relieved by supernatural intervention, bringing the plot full circle thematically with a movement from the demonic to the divine.

Despite this thematic intricacy, "Sir Gowther" is not a sophisticated romance. Probably none of the romances selected for this book is more biased and bloodthirsty than this one, although Sir Launfal's fight with Sir Valentine comes close in terms of the hero's bloodlust. Because it does not lend itself to literary criticism of the older kind, scholars almost completely neglected this romance until recently, mentioning it briefly in comprehensive surveys of English romances and including it in anthologies primarily because its author twice identifies it as a "Breton lay" (lines 28 and 753). With a change in our approach to the study of narrative, however, this romance is now beginning to receive the attention it merits,[1] and, because this interest is recent, even a reader new to the genre may find something worth saying about it that has not been said before. In their essay-length introduction to "Sir Gowther" in which they discuss issues that supplement what is offered here, Anne Laskaya and Eve Salisbury make reference to most of the useful articles available about this romance.[2]

The meter of "Sir Gowther" is the standard tail-rhyme form of twelve-line stanzas, and the poet, like most romance poets, is casual with rhyme and meter. For the most part this modernization is based on the edition by Maldwyn Mills,[3] including his glosses and notes, with help also from the edition by Laskaya and Salisbury.[4] Both editions rely primarily on MS A (Royal), occasionally choosing words or lines from MS B (Advocates), so the present modernization benefits from both versions of the text as well. For ease of reading, the title for the proem and the designation of parts have been provided; these are not in the original text.

---

[1] Jeffrey Jerome Cohen writes interestingly of Gowther's predicament in "Gowther Among the Dogs: Becoming Human c. 1400," *Becoming Male in the Middle Ages*, ed. Jeffrey Jerome Cohen and Bonnie Wheeler (New York: Garland, 1997), 219–44. See also his chapter titled "The Body Hybrid" in *Of Giants* (1999). Other significant studies have followed since.

[2] *The Middle English Breton Lays* (Kalamazoo: TEAMS, 1995), 263–73. The book is also available online. One of the passages of this romance calling for analysis is Gowther's birth story, rich in intertextuality. Within the first hundred lines, the poet appropriates and parodies the stories of Zacharias and Elizabeth and the Annunciation to the Virgin from the Gospel of Luke, and the birth stories of both Merlin and King Arthur, even alluding to a curious passage about semen by Thomas Aquinas. I am grateful to Joy Dorf for alerting me to this wealth of allusion.

[3] *Six Middle English Romances* (London: Dent, 1973), 148–68.

[4] *The Middle English Breton Lays*, 263–307.

Gowther

Proem

Oh God, who art of might the most,
Father, Son and Holy Ghost,
  And paid for Mankind here,
Shield us from the fiend whose role
5 It is to ruin every soul
  At all times of the year!
Once the fiend had power to lie
With ladies, looking to each one's eye
  Just like her husband dear.
10 Thus Merlin he begot, and more,
And made those ladies' hearts so sore
  It's staggering to hear.

Yes, it is strange to hear of fiends
Lying with women, and by that means
15 Getting them with child—
The semen human, for they must take it.
Of themselves they cannot make it,[5]
  Because of Mary mild.
Thus scholars say, and I know how,
20 But won't try to explain it now.
  (Christ keep me undefiled!)[6]
I'll tell you instead of a warlock great
Who caused his mother's heart to break
  With all his deeds so wild.

---

[5] This curious assertion is not folklore but scholarly lore, as the narrator says at line 19. See St. Thomas Aquinas, *Summa Theologica* I.iii, reply to Objection 6.

[6] Apparently fiends "harvest" the semen from men's nocturnal ejaculations. The poet's exclamation in line 21, "As Cryst fro schame me scyld" (Christ shield me from shame), seems to express anxiety about ejaculation, something he knows about but is reluctant to speak of, so here a liberty is taken both to clarify the anxiety being expressed and to improve the rhyme ("undefiled" instead of "shield").

PART I

25   May Jesus Christ in all his glory
       Bless those who love to hear a story
          Of things that once befell.
       Long this Breton lay I sought,
       And out of it a tale I've wrought
30   That lovely is to tell.
       In Austria a duke there dwelt
       Who married a lady, none more svelt
          And comely under kell.[7]
       Bright as a lily was that lady,
35   Bloom on briar no more rosy—
          Excellent damosel!

       When he had married that maiden fair
       And she was duchess, the new-wed pair
          Decided they would make
40   A feast, and knights upon that day
       Jousted in a courtly way
          With many a lance at stake.
       On the next morning nobles went
       To hold a royal tournament[8]
45   For that fair lady's sake.
       The duke himself won fairly ten
       Horses, delighted to fell brave men
          And many a head to break.[9]

       And when this tournament was over,
50   The duke and duchess thought forever
          In joy their lives to lead.
       But ten years passed; with them went joy,
       For he begot, she bore, no boy
          To carry on his seed.
55   So to his lady then he said,

---

[7]   Comely under kell: pretty under her gown, a stock phrase.

[8]   MS A (Royal), which this translation mainly follows, has only a 9-line stanza at this point. Some editors fill in from MS B (Advocates) to make up 12 lines. The TEAMS editors choose to do this, and here the translation follows that edition and their adjusted line numbers throughout the rest of the text.

[9]   The poet intends this as praise of the duke's skill and valor.

"I think a barren wife I've wed;
 Our marriage cannot proceed.
I do but waste my time with thee,
For heirless shall my country be."
60 And then he wept indeed.

The lady sighed so much her face
Lost all its beauty in her disgrace
 That she could not conceive.
She prayed to God and Mary Mild
65 To give her grace to bear a child,
 But how, to them she'd leave.
Then in her orchard one fine day
She met a man who sought to play[10]
 And kisses to receive.
70 As like her lord as he might be,
He laid her down beneath a tree
 Without a by-your-leave.

When he'd done everything he could,
He rose, a hairy fiend, and stood
75 Watching her tremble—and
He said, "I've gotten you with child.
In youth he will be very wild,
 With weapons at his command."
She crossed herself and away she fled
80 Into her chamber, where she said
 (Their room secure and grand)
To her dear lord, that lady mild:
"Tonight we will conceive a child
 To someday rule our land.

85 "An angel came from the heavens bright
And told me so this very night,
 God's messenger, I believe.
He said that it would end our strife."
So by her gown he caught his wife:
90 "Let's try then to conceive."
The two did not then hesitate.

---

[10] "Play" often has a sexual meaning in medieval romance. (Cp. modern English "foreplay.")

The duke embraced his lovely mate
　　Upon that very eve.
He played with that most gracious lady,
But she would carry the devil's baby
　　Till God gave her reprieve.

This child within her was none other
Than our Lord Merlin's own half-brother.
　　One fiend sired both boys, for
They all are interested in
Tempting young girls to the sin
　　Of being a devil's whore.
The duchess then grew bigger fast
Until she had a child at last
　　Who'd torment rich and poor.
The duke had him taken speedily
And christened "Gowther"[11]—yet he'd be
　　Fierce as a wild boar.

But now the duke consoled his lady.
He ordered wet nurses for the baby,
　　The best in the whole countree.
The baby suckled with all his might
The wives of many an excellent knight,
　　And soon he had slain three!
The child was young and fast he grew.
The duke quickly found six more to do
　　The suckling, and listen to me—
Well before twelve months were gone
He'd slain nine nursemaids, one by one,
　　Ladies highborn and free.

Knights of that land, assembling, spoke.
They told the duke it was no joke
　　To lose their wives that way:
"Do something else to feed that boy.
He'll take no more of his former joy
　　In wet nurses from today."
His mother suffered a nasty shock

95

100

105

110

115

120

125

---

[11]　This sounds like a significant name, but the dictionaries are not helpful about a possible meaning.

The day she took him up to rock:
    He turned his head her way
130   And ripped the nipple from her breast.
Backwards she fell and called a priest,
    And fled her baby boy!

Physicians quickly mended her,
But women then reluctant were
135   To let young Gowther near.
They fed him up with bread and meat,
As much of that as he would eat.
    He thrived on it, I swear.
And when he was fifteen years old,
140   He made a weapon he could hold
    But no one else could bear:
A falchion made of steel and iron.[12]
You may be sure he was very strong,
    And everyone feared him there.

145   Then in one twelve-month, more he grew
Than most in six or seven do
    And soon was ready to go
On horseback, but his ways were grim.
The duke did not dare chastise him
150   And made him a knight, although
Nobody there in all the land
Dared to raise a restraining hand
    To curb his falchion's blow.
Soon for sorrow the duke was dead,
155   And then the mother a sad life led.
    She could not hide her woe.

More sorrow she could not endure,
So to a limestone castle, her
    Own property, she fled.
160   She made it strong, took refuge there.
Her men might tell of sorrow and care,
    For ill they were bestead.[13]

---

[12] This weapon, a type of sword possibly curved, now becomes thematically associated with Gowther throughout the romance.

[13] Ill bestead: in a bad situation.

When they met Gowther along the way,
"It was an evil thing," they'd say,
165   "That child was ever fed,"
For with his falchion, knights he slew
And cut their noble steeds in two—
    Such perils filled them with dread.

By now a duke of great renown,
170 Men of the Church would he strike down,
    Whenever they came near.
No mass or matins would he hire
Or preaching by any holy friar,
    This I truly swear.
175 But early and late and loud and still,
He'd always work his father's will
    Wherever he might fare.[14]
Of all things he loved hunting best,
In park, in woods, in wilderness,
180   At all times, everywhere.

He went out hunting one fine day,
And seeing a convent along the way,
    Toward it he turned to ride.
The prioress and her nuns all came
185 With grand procession out to him
    Full hastily that noontide,
For of his body they were afraid—
And rightly: he and his men first laid
    With them, and then (why hide
190 The truth?) he locked them in their kirk[15]
And burnt them up. This sort of work
    Was talked of far and wide.

To young and old who had belief
In Christ, he caused the greatest grief
195   That he could think to do.
He'd spoil the hopes of a maid to wed,[16]
And rape a young wife in her bed,

---

14   I.e., he'd do the devil's work wherever he went.

15   Kirk: church.

16   I.e., destroy her virginity.

And slay her husband too,
And over cliffs old monks he'd drive
200   And hang up priests on hooks, alive,
And others he merely slew.
To burn up hermits he thought a game;
He set a poor old widow aflame,
And those who escaped were few.

PART II

205   At last an old earl of that land
Went to the young duke to demand,
"Sir, why do you so?
We doubt you've Christian ancestry
And think some fiend's son you must be,
210   To cause such bitter woe.
You do no good, but always evil.
We think you're close kin to the devil."
This angered Gowther so,
In fury he said, "If you lie to me,
215   Hanged and quartered you shall be.
Alive you'll never go!"

He ordered the earl in prison cast
And went to his mother's fort as fast
As ever he could ride.
220   "Mother," he said, "now tell me quick
Who was my father? Don't misspeak,
Or through you this shall glide!"
(His falchion was pointed at her breast.)
"And if you love your health, you'd best
225   Speak fast!" "My lord who died,"
She answered him, "your father was."
And then his tears began, because,
"I think," he said, "you've lied."

"Well, son, since I the truth must say,
230   Down in our orchard one fine day
A fiend begot you, for,
As like my lord as he could be,
He took me under a chestnut tree."

And then they both wept sore.
235 "Go quickly, mother, and confess.
I'm off to Rome before I rest,
To learn another lore."[17]
This thought had come with a sudden sigh,
And "Mercy, Lord!" he began to cry
240 To God whom Mary bore.[18]

He prayed that from his father the fiend
God and Mary, who is the queen
Of mercy granted free,
Would save and bring him to that bliss
245 God bought for all of us with His
Torment upon the Tree.[19]
Then he went home and, calling to
The earl, he openly said, "How true
The tale was you told me.
250 To Rome I'll go where the apostle[20]
May shrive and cleanse me, and my castle
I'll leave, good earl, with thee."

So with the earl remaining there
To be his most reliable heir,
255 Gowther began to stride
Toward Rome. He also sometimes ran,
Desiring neither horse nor man
With him to run or ride.
He had his falchion with him still.
260 He left it not, for good or ill.
It hung always by his side.
To Rome went Gowther full of hope,

---

[17] He advises her to go to make confession to a priest, while he will go to Rome to find another way of being (lore), which will involve contrition (being sorry about his past misdeeds) and penance. The suddenness of this conversion can be justified both psychologically, as the discovery that one's parents are not whom one has always thought is deeply traumatic, and historically, by the precedent of Saint Paul's equally sudden conversion on the road to Damascus, from persecutor of the early Christians to identity with them (Acts 9).

[18] In this and other medieval works God and Jesus (whom Mary bore) are firmly believed to be one Person.

[19] Tree: i.e., the Cross.

[20] The apostle: the Pope, who will shrive Gowther, that is, "cleanse" him of his sins.

But there, before he met the Pope,
   Full long he had to bide.

265   And when at last allowed to see
   The Pope, he went down on his knee
     And greeted him, and soon
   Was praying in humble adoration
   Both for shrift and absolution.
270   On granting him his boon,
   The Pope asked, "Where are you from, what land?"
   "I'm Duke of Austria," said the man,
     "By God true on his throne.
   There a fiend became my father,
275   Betraying the duchess who's my mother.
     Of friends, my father has none."

   "I'll help," the Pope said. "Did your other
   Father christen you?" "Yes, 'Gowther'—
     That's the name I bear."
280   "I praise God that you've now come hither,
   Or I'd have had to travel thither
     With my men of war,
   For holy churches you've destroyed."
   "Nay, father, do not be annoyed,
285   For truly," Gowther swore,
   "Now at thy bidding shall I be.
   I'll keep the penance[21] you lay on me
     And never harm Christians more."

   "Lay down your falchion, then," said he.
290   "Confess before I leave,[22] and be
     Absolved." But Gowther then
   Said, "Nay, holy father. It remains
   Always with me, for my friends
     Are few and far between."
295   "Then you must travel north and south,
   And only food that's from the mouth
     Of a dog may you take in,
   And speak no word of good or ill,

---

[21] Penance: voluntary suffering to show repentance.
[22] Leave: i.e., before the Pope goes to war.

And wait for the sign from God that will
300   Show He forgives your sin."

Gowther knelt to the Pope, resolved,
And solemnly the Pope absolved
    The knight that very day.
But then he got no food in Rome
305 Except from one dog's mouth a bone,
    And quickly went his way.
He went out from that city, and
Traveled into a distant land,
    As those who report it say.
310 When near a hill he took his seat,
A greyhound brought him there his meat[23]
    Around the close of day.

PART III

For three nights Gowther chose to stay.
The greyhound came there every day,
315   And a good white loaf he brought.
Upon the fourth no dog came, though,
So Gowther then got up to go,
    And loved God in his thought.
He came to a castle by the road.
320 It was an emperor's abode,
    And thitherward he sought
The way, then sat outside the gate.
He dared do nothing then but wait—
    Which was just what he ought.

325 The guards blew trumpets on the wall
And knights then gathered in the hall.
    The lord went to his seat.
Sir Gowther rose and went inside.
No usher at the door he spied
330   Nor porter did he meet,
So in as swift as he was able
He went on through to the hall's high table

---

[23] Meat: i.e., food.

And dove near the royal feet.
The steward came with stick in hand
335   To drive him out, with a sharp command,
Threatening he would beat

Him fiercely unless he went away.
"What is it?" he heard the emperor say.
The steward answered, "It's
340   The handsomest man I've ever seen.
Come look! He's crouching there between
The dogs. Look—there he sits!"
From Gowther nary a word would come.
The emperor said he must be dumb
345   Or else had lost his wits.
"And yet perchance it may be true
That it's a penance he has to do."
Sometimes on the truth one hits.

The emperor, seated again, was served,
350   And noble knights his dinner carved.
He sent the man a share.
But Gowther left it, wanting none.
Along came a spaniel with a bone
And bore it under where
355   Sir Gowther sat. Away the flawed
Knight pulled it, and he greedily gnawed,
Wishing no finer fare.
Bodily sustenance wanted he none
But what he from a dog's mouth won,
360   Even if gnawed on there.

The emperor, and the empress, too,
And ladies and knights on the dais who
Were watching what he did,
Gave to their hounds a lot of meat.
365   Among the dogs he would only eat,
But amply was he fed.
Then from the hounds when he had eaten,
To a small room he was taken
And under a drape he hid.
370   Whenever he then came to the hall,

"Hob our Fool" is what they'd call
Him who did as God bid.

PART IV

It happened that this emperor
Had a daughter fair as a flower,
375   But dumb as Gowther. She
Wished to speak and never could.
But she was beautiful and good,
     And courtly as could be.
A messenger came to them one day
380 And to her father had this to say:
     "My lord sends greetings. He
Who sultan is of greatest might
Says he will harry you day and night,
     Burn buildings utterly,

385 And slay your gallant men, unless
Your daughter, fair and courteous,
     You send him at once, to wed."
The emperor said, "I've one alone,
And she is dumb as any stone,
390   Though none is better bred.
And I shall *never*, by Christ, be found
Giving my girl to a heathen hound!
     The sorrow would strike me dead.
Yet Holy God may, through his might,
395 Someday teach her to talk all right."
     Away the messenger sped—

Straight to the sultan and told him this,
And that was the end of peace and bliss.
     The heathen host[24] drew near.
400 The emperor, valiant under shield,
Engaged the enemy in the field.
     Of battle he had no fear.
Gowther went to his room apart
And fervently prayed that God, who bought

---

[24] Host: i.e., army.

405   Him on the Cross so dear,[25]
            Would send him, to help his lord, a horse,
            And, to sustain him there, of course,
               Send armor, shield and spear.

            Hardly had he made this prayer
410   Than horse and armor both were there
               Outside the chamber door,
            And both of them were colored black.
            He leaped upon the stallion's back
               That stalwart was, and bore
415   His shield upon his shoulder strong,
            And took his spear up, big and long,
               To spur through mire and moor.[26]
            And when the knight came galloping through
            The gates, none but the maiden knew
420   Who after her father tore.

            The emperor had an army keen,
            The sultan another. Each had been
               Arranged into a row.
            Sir Gowther through the Saracens went
425   And many a helmet did he dent.
               He struck down many a foe
            And caused to stagger enemies' steeds.
            Their brave hearts faltered when his deeds
               Set blood and brains aflow.
430   He smote off many a heathen's head,
            And out of their saddles they tumbled, dead
               And hacked from head to toe.

            He put the sultan himself to flight
            And made the chase last into night
435   As Saracens he slew.
            Then home ahead of the emperor
            He rode, and only that dumb and fair
               Maiden ever knew.
            He went to his room and there disarmed,
440   And horse and armor away were charmed

---

[25] Dear is an adverb meaning at great cost, i.e., with his life.

[26] Mire and moor: i.e., bog and heath, rough terrain.

Somewhere beyond his view.
He found his lord in the hall at meat
And under the table took his seat
Next to a dog or two.

445   The maiden took two greyhounds fine
And washed their mouths out clean with wine
And put a loaf in one
And into the other excellent pork.
He welcomed both and went to work,[27]
450   Strong in body and bone.
He sat at ease at the emperor's feet
Then to his room made his retreat
Where he could be alone.
With bad news for the emperor,
455   The messenger returned, before
The night was fully gone.

"Sir," he said, "I bring a letter.
My lord comes here to know you better.
You slew his favorite men
460   All yesterday, so to the field
He brings today, with spear and shield,
A thousand more than ten.
Thus shall he be avenged on you!"
"Armor," the lord said, "horses, too,
465   We'd better assemble, then."
Now God sent Gowther, through His might,
A red horse and red armor bright.
He followed through firth and fen.[28]

Once the battlelines were arrayed,
470   Truly, as the romance has said,
Gowther rode in between.
Many a knight he caused to stumble
And head over tail made horses tumble.
It was an amazing scene!
475   Helmet and shield he hewed asunder,
And cut down banners that were a wonder

---

[27] Work: i.e., eating them.

[28] Firth and fen: woods and marsh.

Of brilliance and sheen.
Laying upon those Saracens dark,
He cracked their helmets all apart,
480   Thus proving he was keen.

"Holy God!" said the emperor,
"What knight is that, so bold in war,
       And all arrayed in red?
Red are his armor and his steed.
485   He's making many a heathen bleed,
       And striking others dead.
Hither he's come to help me out.
Another knight yesterday rode about
       Fighting in black, instead,
490   Defeating sultan and Saracen
As yonder knight does, downing men
       With blows as heavy as lead.

"Strong his falchion is with steel.
Look how his blows make Saracens reel.
495   He never wastes a one!"
Into the press when Gowther heard
The emperor speak, he to him spurred,
       Belaboring flesh and bone.
Soon the sultan to a forest fled
500   And all his host with him he led,
       Those few who could carry on.
Sir Gowther turned his bridle at last.
Ahead of his lord he galloped fast
       And into his room was gone.

505   When once his armor was undone,
His horse and it were quickly gone
       Away, he knew not where.
And when he came into the hall,
The emperor and his men were all
510   Eating their dinner there.
Among the dogs he hunkered down,
And then the maiden fetched a hound

And acted unaware[29]—
Fed "Hob the Fool," that is to say,
515   Just as she had the previous day,
In under-the-table lair.

The emperor thanked our God in Heaven
(Who made our days and nights, all seven)
For good luck, as he said,
520   In overcoming the sultan twice
And slaying the enemy—that was nice—
Except for those that fled.
"Because a strange knight came to us
Each day, we were victorious,
525   Wherever they're from. In red
The one was armored, the other in black,
And if of either there'd been a lack,
We'd have been ill bestead."[30]

Trumpets were blowing in the hall
530   And knights and ladies dancing, all
Before that minstrelsy.[31]
Sir Gowther in his chamber lay.
He did not want to dance or play,
So very tired was he,
535   Bruised by the blows that he'd received
When in the battle he'd sorely grieved
Many an enemy.
He had no thought but of his sin
And how the salvation he might win
540   That God bought on the Tree.

Soon those lords were ready for bed,
And knights and ladies, too, it's said
In this romance of old.
A messenger came to the emperor
545   At dawn and said, "Now there'll be war.
Your sorrow shall be cold.
My lord is coming with all his power.

---

[29]   She pretends not to know that he is the red knight.

[30]   Ill bestead: in a bad situation.

[31]   Minstrelsy: music of minstrels.

Unless you give him daughter and dower,
    The strongest castle you hold
550   He'll take. He'll thrash you blood and bone
And leave alive not a single one
    Of all your barons bold!"

"I scorn his threats," said the emperor,
"For I've got men as good at war.
555   I'll fight him right away."
The warriors that to him belonged
Armed quickly and around him thronged
    By noontime of that day.
Mounting, they took up shield and spear,
560   And when good Gowther came to hear
    Of this, he knelt to pray
That horse and armor the Deity might
Send him. Both came soon, milk-white.
    He rode in good array.

565   The dumb girl twice had seen him go,
And now again. None other could know
    But God that it was he.
Going with neither brag nor boast,
Quickly he galloped after the host
570   And followed where he could see
The emperor, who his army led.
Sir Gowther galloped out ahead,
    His courage exemplary.
The barons were being hacked apart,
575   But now each one with all his heart
    Struck back more valiantly.

On the black banner that went before
The sultan, three rampant[32] lions were
    Embroidered, of silver hue.
580   One was crowned with crimson red,
Another crowned with gold instead,
    The third one crowned with blue.
His helmet also was very rich,

---

[32] Rampant: standing with claws outstretched.

Inlaid with carbuncle rubies, which
585   Were ringed with diamonds too.
For battle finely he was arrayed
With his broad banner on parade,
      But soon great harm he knew.

Gowther, the good repentant knight,
590   Mightily fought in gear of white,
      None braver, I would say,
And every blow from Gowther's hand
Would fell a horse or a heathen man
      And cut through a helmet gray.[33]
595   When knights went tumbling to the ground,
Soldiers on foot no courage found
      And madly ran away.
The sultan, who for the emperor's daughter
Caused such Christian and heathen slaughter,
600   Had reason to curse the day.

And always Gowther fought and raced,
And many a valiant horse he chased
      To death, so he could reach
A foe; and those his falchion struck
605   Fell to the ground, beyond the luck
      Of help from any leech.[34]
But he would not, in anger or threat,
Utter a word—no, not yet—
      For fear of God, and each
610   Time he hungered, nothing he ate
But what he might from a dog's mouth take,
      Obeying the Papal speech.

Sir Gowther in his armor glowed
And always with the emperor rode,
615   Protecting him from harm.
There was no Saracen great of strength
Who dared to come within spear's-length,
      So strong were they both of arm,
And with his falchion long and curved,

---

[33] Gray: the helmets are of steel.

[34] Leech: doctor.

620 Heavy the blows Sir Gowther served.
    Their lives held little charm
For those who dared to stand their ground
Where certain death would soon be found.
    His blows came in a swarm.

625 Gowther was fully engaged in the fight.
The emperor, too, with all his might,
    But suddenly he was gone—
Caught by the foe! With falchion's edge,
Gowther demanded the sultan's pledge:[35]
630   His head, struck it off anon,[36]
And rescued his lord. This made him glad
Because in his heart he so loved God
    Who made us, blood and bone.
But then a spear with a horrible hiss
635 Went through his shoulder. Seeing this,
    The dumb girl uttered a moan ...

PART V

Then from her tower the emperor's daughter
Fell, in the sorrow that blow brought her,
    ·Knowing it struck her knight.
640 A valiant squire took care of her,
But for two days she did not stir.
    Death seemed to be her plight.
The lord came home and sat at the table.
Gowther, as soon as he was able
645   (Much wounded in the fight),
Went to his chamber, took off his gear,
And went to dinner. When he was there,
    He missed the maiden bright.

But from the dogs he won his meat.
650 The emperor, sober after his sweet
    And gracious daughter's fall,
Sent earls and barons to Rome to bring
The Pope to bury that sweet thing.

---

[35] Pledge: an item to be redeemed (normally).

[36] Anon: at once.

With many a cardinal,
655 He came to assoil the maiden and bless,
But God sent to the girl a grace
    Quite inexplicable,
As much to everyone's surprise
She stretched, and spoke in phrases wise
660   To Gowther, over them all.

She said, "My Lord of Heaven sends,
Through me, his greetings, and he intends
    Forgiveness for you, and bliss.
He bids you speak now without fear,
665 And eat, drink and make merry here,
    For you are one of his."
And then she said to her father, "He
Who fought beside you on all three
    Days of battle—is this!"
670 The Pope shrived Gowther thoroughly,
And, praising God and Mary, he
    Bestowed the Papal kiss.

He said, "Of God you are the child.
No longer fear the warlock wild,[37]
675   For vanquished now is he."
Then with consent of the emperor
And Pope, Sir Gowther married her
    Who had so courteously
Behaved, the lady good and fair
680 Who of her father's lands was heir;
    A better there could not be!
The Pope then took his leave to go.
He'd given the pair his blessing, so
    Away to Rome went he.

685 When all the festivities were spent,
Sir Gowther back to Austria went.
    He gave the old earl all
His power over that countree
And let him marry his mother, she

---

[37] Warlock wild: here, the devil.

as and small.[38]
hat he endowed
, and avowed
ed, "I shall
erein he placed
ad and sing for the grace
that wall.

e Pope had shriven
his sins forgiven,
as sore
hings he'd done,
with many a nun
convent poor.
by a river
d it forever
ray there for
s this world turned,
he had burned,
evermore.

back home again,
got to Allemagne,[40]
was dead.
d emperor,
ian knights the flower,
s' dread.
him, in God's name,
aid for them.
he fed.
rful get what's right,
with all his might,
he led.

(naming him
al person who
and prose that
describes him
ing the clearly
English saint
of Orpheus as

om Austria (see line 272), "home" (line 709) is

Reigning there for many a year,
He was a powerful emperor
  And wisely ruled the land.
And when he died, it's true to say,
725 They buried him in the very way
  That he himself had planned.
He was a saintly man and true,
And Christians call him "Guthlac,"[41] who
  By God's most holy hand
730 Does miracles, for firm his hold
On faith was. Now in a shrine of gold
  He lies, a blessed man.

Whoever seeks God faithfully
For suffering finds a remedy.
735   God promises this right
So that no one need despair.
The Holy Ghost inspired there
  Gowther, the cursèd knight,
And now he makes the blind to see
740 And dumb to speak, through God, and he
  Makes all that's crooked right.
He gives the madman back his wits
And does more miracles, and it's
  All through God's grace and might.

755 Thus Sir Gowther recovered, for
First he was powerful, then was poor,
  Then mighty again one day.
Though he was fathered by a fiend,
Grace for a better life he gleaned,
750   For God showed him the way.
Written on parchment this story was,
And it's so excellent because

---

[41] This bizarre identification of Gowther with Guthlac occurs only in MS
Gotlake). Saint Guthlac, a royal warrior who became a hermit, was a r
lived in East Anglia around AD 700 He inspired biographies in both vers
describe a life very different from Gowther's. *The Oxford Dictionary of Sain*
as "one of the most important pre-Conquest saints of England" (85). Identi
European Gowther (Austrian-born in the romance; see lines 271–72) with t
is a ploy reminiscent of the "Orfeo" poet's strange identification of the Thra
Winchester in order to relocate that story to England.

It's from a Breton lay.
May Jesus Christ, who's God's son, give

755   Us strength with that great Lord to live
Whose might is most,[42] we pray.
             Amen.

---

[42] Cp. the first line of the romance.

CHAPTER 9

Floris and Blancheflour

This romance of young love (very young love, though the age of these "children" seems to vary from scene to scene) is the second-oldest English romance extant, retold c. 1250 from an earlier and much longer French version of around 1160. Apparently of Near Eastern origin, the plot about devoted lovers of opposing religions was extremely popular in the middle ages, and versions of this story exist in all the major languages of Western Europe. In that feature, as well as its "oriental" setting, highly elaborated in the description of the harem-tower, the story bears some resemblance to the French *chante-fable* (tale with song) of "Aucassin and Nicolette," about a young Christian prince who loves an enterprising Saracen maiden.[1] Both romances have been presented as plays with great success, and both construct the "Eastern Other" in a way very different

---

[1] The French "Aucassin and Nicolette" is charmingly related in quasi-archaic prose, with the songs in verse, by the great teller of fairy tales, Andrew Lang. Roger Sherman Loomis and Laura Hibbard Loomis include his version with their own prose retellings of other stories in *Medieval Romances* (New York: Modern Library, 1957).

from the wicked Saracens of such Middle English romances as, for example, "Sir Gowther." The angry Saracen amyral reminds us, more than anyone else among these nine romances, of angry King Arthur in "Sir Launfal."

Like "Emaré," but more abundantly, "Floris and Blancheflour" relies on repetitions of lines that function as refrains, a practice that may puzzle and annoy the modern reader unless alerted ahead of time. At least eight such refrains emphasize themes in the poem, and one might imagine these as being half-sung like the more explicit refrains of a French *chante-fable*. The poet relies on four-stress rhymed couplets, with both stress and rhyme being rather loose in the original. Pronunciation of names also is variable in the original: "Blancheflour" is pronounced sometimes with two sylla-bles and sometimes with three, "Floris" may be stressed on either syllable, depending on the poet's need, and the "-flour" element of Blancheflour's name can rhyme with either "flower" or "door." I am grateful for this flex-ibility and make use of it in my translation. The text used for this trans-lation is Robert D. Stevick's edition in *Five Middle English Narratives* (Indianapolis: The Bobbs-Merrill Company, 1967), which he bases on the Egerton manuscript with a few additions from the Auchinleck manuscript. The translation additionally twice follows Cambridge manuscript variants in Stevick's notes.

The story is set in three locations: Almeria in Islamic Spain, briefly in Montargis in France, and in Babylon. All three are real places as well as romance sites.[2] The movement from one place to another is indicated in the translation by inserted subtitles.

All four English manuscripts of "Floris and Blancheflour" have a fragmentary beginning, but the first part of the story may be summarized from the French version as follows:

> The Saracen ruler of the land of Almeria (in what is now south-ern Spain) has captured a Christian woman on a raid. On the day of the Festival of Flowers, known to English-speakers as Palm Sunday, she gives birth to a daughter. The queen of Almeria gives birth to a son on the same day. Because they are

---

[2] Although the actual existence and geographical location of these three places are of little or no importance to the English romance (in which Babylon, for example, is made a seaside city), they will be of interest to some readers: Almería remains a province of southern Spain, dominated by the city of the same name, an important seaport on the Mediterranean that was founded by Abd ar-Rahman II of Cordoba in 955. It remained "Saracen" until the days of Ferdinand and Isabella, to whom the Moors surrendered it in 1486, and it is now an important Spanish resort site. Montargis is a city of canals and bridges not far south of Paris in central France, still medieval in its charm. Babylon, now in ruins, lies about 55 miles south of Baghdad, very much inland in central Iraq.

born on this festival, the girl is called Blancheflour and the boy Floris. The Christian woman has the care of both children and nurses them together.

Part I

IN ALMERIA (SPAIN)

No one need seek a sweeter pair
Of children living anywhere.
The Christian woman nursed the two
And loved them both, as mothers do,
5   And both together long she fed;
For seven years that life they led.[3]
The king then came one day to see
His son, and said that it would be
A very grievous thing indeed
10   Unless his boy would learn to read
The Latin letters—whole books, too,
As men both high and low must do.
"And since you *must* learn, son," said he,
Be sure to do it earnestly."
15   But then the little boy replied,
As standing before the king he cried,
And weeping asked him mournfully,
"Shall Blancheflour not then learn with me?
For I cannot learn anything
20   Without Blancheflour. I cannot sing
My lessons[4] or learn how to read
Without Blancheflour," he said. "Indeed?"
The king replied to his son in turn.
"For thy love, then, the girl shall learn."
25   Thus did the two their schooling start,
And each of the children was so smart
That seeing them learn a wonder was.
Their love was yet more marvelous;
The children loved each other so
30   That never apart would either go.
When five years in the school they'd been,
So well the pair had learned by then,

---

[3]   Although in some cultures long nursing is acceptable, more likely this merely means that the two children were free of responsibility, considered "infants" in the British sense, for seven years.

[4]   Many recitations were sung in medieval schools in order to ease their memorization, a purpose served by our modern alphabet song.

That each of them their Latin knew,
Both how to read, and write it, too.

35 The king, who saw his boy's love for
The little maiden Blancheflour,
Worried that when they came of age
Good common sense might not assuage
Their love. His son might not withdraw
40 His love when he should wed by law.
So therefore to the queen he went
To tell her their predicament
And of his great concern and care
About his son, how he would fare.
45 "Dame," he said, "my advice herewith
Is soon to put Blancheflour to death,
For once that maiden has been slain,
Her days cut short so none remain,
When Floris knows it has been done,
50 He'll soon forget her and move on,
And then more properly he will wed."

The queen replied to him and said
(Thinking that the advice she gave
Might serve the maiden's life to save),
55 "It might be, sir, to more effect
To make sure Floris has respect
And that he not lose honor for
The death of maiden Blancheflour.
Better to take her far away
60 Than order some poor soul to slay
The child. More honorable that would be
Than killing her. Don't you agree?"
The king said that it might be true,
But with unease. "What should we do?"
65 "Sire, our Floris we should send
To Montargis, that he might spend
Time with my sister, who will be
Pleased, as that country's lady, to see
Our son, and she will understand
70 Why we have sent him from our land,
And she'll attempt with all her might,

Both in the daytime and by night,
To curb his love for Blancheflour
As if that passion never were."
Then, "Sir," she said, "I've had another
Thought: we should persuade her mother
That she pretend to the girl to be
So sick that it explains why she
Cannot from her mother's bedside go."

75

Now both these children are full of woe
Because they cannot be together.
More sorrowful have they been never.
Young Floris wept before the king:
"Oh, sir, it hurts like anything,
Your plan to send me far away
When my dear Blancheflour must stay.
Now that we can't together be,
My joy has turned to misery!"
The king said gently, "Floris, I'm
Sure that within a fortnight's time,
Whether her mother lives or dies,
I'm positive we can devise
A way that maid shall come to you."
"Yes, sir," said Floris. "I pray it's true,
For if you send her there to me,
Then I don't care where I shall be."
The king, glad they'd agreed again,
Entrusted him to his chamberlain.

80

85

90

95

IN MONTARGIS (FRANCE)

With fanfare appropriate to one
Who was a mighty ruler's son,
They greeted him kindly, Duke Orgás,
The man who king of that castle was,
And Floris' aunt. But ever were
The thoughts of Floris on Blancheflour.
Glad and blithe they were with him,
But everything he saw seemed dim;
Nothing could cheer him, song or game,
Until the day his dear one came.

100

105

His aunt set him to learning where
110   The other little children were,
Both girls and boys, for Montargis
Draws many where good learning is.
But Floris sighs and nothing learns,
And for Blancheflour forever yearns.
115   If anyone speaks to him apart,
Love is so fastened in his heart,
Love at his heart's root so complete,
That nothing else can seem so sweet.
Not galingale[5] or licorice
120   Is half so sweet as her love is—
Nor anything, no root or flower.
He thinks so much of his Blancheflour
That one day seems as long as three,
When he may not his dear love see.
125   So thus he lived immersed in grief,
And with the fortnight went belief
That she was coming. When he knew
That she was not, his sorrow grew
So great he could not eat or drink
130   Or close his eyes to sleep a wink.
The chamberlain wrote to the king
Informing him of everything.

BACK IN ALMERIA

Quickly the king broke through the seal
To see what the letter would reveal,
135   But he began to change his mood
As very soon he understood,
And angrily he called his queen
To tell the contretemps there'd been.
Truly annoyed, "Now bring," he said,
140   "The maiden here! Now off her head,
As you should understand, must go!"
But then the queen was full of woe,
And this she said, that gentle lady:
"For God's love, show the girl some mercy!

---

5   Galingale: a sweet spice.

145   Down at the harbor, there below,
Are wealthy merchants, this I know,
Coming from Babylon, very rich
And glad to make a purchase which
Goes up in value. Thus you may
150   Exchange her for fine goods as pay.
Better that from us she be bought
Than slay her, when we'd rather not."
With some misgivings, the king said he'd
Accept her counsel, and agreed.
155   So for a burgess[6] then he sent,
A man both courteous and intent
On how most profitably to sell,
And languages he knew as well.
Soon was the maiden by that warder
160   Taken down to the nearby harbor,
And there to those rich merchants sold
For twenty marks of gleaming gold,
Along with a cup so good and rich
In all the world there was not its match.
165   Never was finer goblet made.
The artist, no mere knave, portrayed
Upon that cup the famous scene
Where Paris led away the queen,[7]
And on the lid that lay above
170   Portrayed was their illicit love.
Set in the knob on top there shone
A carbuncle,[8] an enormous stone,
And nowhere was so deep a cellar
It wouldn't light up, so that a fellow
175   Could fill his jug with ale or wine
To pour into golden vessels fine.
Aeneas in Trojan battle won
The cup, and when the war was done,
He took it into Lombardy

---

[6] Burgess: a commercial inhabitant of a city (burg).

[7] Paris's abduction of Helen of Troy instigated the Trojan War.

[8] Carbuncle: a deep red gem of the East Indies.

180 And gave it to his dear *amie*.[9]
Then someone stole it. A thief in Rome
Robbed Caesar's treasure and took it home,
And later he exchanged it for
The purchasing of Blancheflour.
185 He thought to triple the goblet's worth
By bringing her to his land of birth.

IN BABYLON

These merchants sailed across the ocean,
Taking the maiden to their nation.
When they had sailed both far and long,
190 At last they came to Babylon,[10]
And to the *amyral*[11] of that place
They sold that maiden of lovely face.
He bought her without thinking twice,
Quickly agreeing on the price,
195 And for her, standing straight and bold,
Gave seven times her weight in gold!
He thought, as soon as he had seen
The girl, to take her as his queen,
And placed her in his royal tower
200 With honor in the maidens' bower,
And there those merchants left the maid,
Well-pleased with profit from their trade.
Now let us also leave Blancheflour,
And speak of Floris, home once more.[12]

IN ALMERIA

205 Back went the burgess to the king
In order the payment of gold to bring,
And in his treasury the king locked up
All the coins and the golden cup.

---

[9] *Amie* (French): beloved. According to Virgil's *Aeneid*, after the Trojan War ended, Aeneas made his way to Italy to found Rome, where he married Lavinia. The legendary history implicit in lines 177–80 is that Aeneas gave this splendid cup to his bride.

[10] Babylon: This ancient city, in what is now Iraq, was entirely landbound.

[11] *Amyral*: emir, overlord (the source of our word "admiral").

[12] This story-marker signals an interlacing of two plots that occur at once.

Within a church he ordered made
210   A tomb as an elaborate grave.
He ordered them to lay thereon
A fair and newly painted stone,
And all around it letters were
Carved in honor of Blancheflour,
215   And anybody could have read
How those words spoke and what they said:
"Here below lies sweet Blancheflour
That Floris loved so *par amour*."[13]

Now Floris, sailing back for home,
220   Soon to his father's hall has come.
As soon as Floris comes in sight,
His father greets him with delight,
His mother happily greets him, too,
But it is all that Floris can do
225   To keep from asking for Blancheflour.
When he can't wait there any more,
He leaves the chamber at a run
And into her mother's room has come,
And to her mother there he said,
230   Where is Blancheflour, my sweet maid?"
"Oh, sir," she said, "forsooth, Floris,
I don't know where my daughter is."
Thus she remembered to say the lie
The king had told her she must try.
235   But Floris said, "Don't mock me so.
Your lying gives me too much woe.
Just tell me where my lover is!"
Then weeping she replied with this:
"Sir, dead," she said. "Dead!" said he.
240   "Oh, sir," she said, "It's true, you see."
"Alas, when did that sweet girl die?"
"Sir, within this fortnight. I
Myself saw earth being laid above
Her body, dead, and for thy love."
245   This so shocked Floris, fair and noble,
He swooned right there and tumbled over.

---

[13] *Par amour* (French): as lover. Compare the derived English word "paramour," but of course the children's love is not sexual (at this point).

The woman, thinking he might die,
Began on Jesus and Mary to cry.
Hearing her wail, the queen and king
250   Into her room came hastening.
The queen saw, lying there before
Her very eyes, the child she bore.
The king's heart, too, was brimful of
Regret to see him torn by love.
255   But Floris revived. He was not dead.
He wept and sorely sighed, and said
To his mother the queen, "I pray,
Please take me to her, right away."
Thither they brought him quickly, lest
260   He die for sorrow. It was best
That to behold her grave he came,
And there he saw it, with her name,
And when the inscription he had read,
All the letters and what they said—
265   "Here below lies sweet Blancheflour
That Floris loved so, *par amour*"—
He fainted three times in a row
And could not speak at first, although
As soon as he awoke, he crept
270   Beside her grave and sorely wept
And sighed, "White Flower! My White Flower!
A sweeter thing was never in bower!
For you, Blancheflour, I now lament,
A lady of such fine descent.
275   Everyone, small and great, loved you
For all your goodness, and beauty too.
If death were only apportioned right,
We both would die in a single night,
Just as we on a single day
280   Were born." Then he went on to say,
"Oh, Death, of envy you're so full,
You brimmed with treachery until
You had to steal away my lover.
Truly, you were jealous of her.
285   To let her live you did not dare,
And I shall die, and you don't care.
Therefore no more on Death I'll call,

But kill myself for once and all!"
He drew his knife out of the sheath
290 And would have stabbed himself to death—
Yes, to his heart he would have plunged
The knife—had not his mother lunged
At him to stop what was about
To happen, wrenched the dagger out
295 Of his clenched fist, and hurled that knife
Away, and saved her poor son's life!

The queen now, having stopped that danger,
Ran straight into the royal chamber
Where the king was, and the lady
300 Cried, "For God's love, sir, have mercy!
Of our twelve children now there's none
That's still alive except this one,
And better were Blancheflour his mate
Than that he perish for her sake!"
305 "You're right, my lady," said the king,
"And since there is no other thing
To do, I'd rather she were his wife
Than that my dear son lose his life."
The queen, by these words filled with joy,
310 Ran back at once to tell her boy:
"Floris, be happy now, for I've
Made sure you'll see your love alive.
Floris, my son, through trickery
Both by your father and by me,
315 We had this grave, an empty one,
Constructed for your sake, dear son,
So you'd forget that girl you knew
And take the wife we wanted for you."
Then every word to him she told
320 Of how the maiden had been sold.
"Then is this true, my mother dear?"
"Truly," she said, "she is not here."
That rough memorial stone they took
Away from the grave and let him look:
325 No maid was there! "Mother, I may
Live now," he said. "But night or day
I shall not rest a single hour

Until I've found my sweet Blancheflour,
And I must even seek my friend,
330   If need be, to the world's far end!"

Now Floris bid the king of Spain,
His father, farewell—who said, "Remain."
"No, sir," said Floris, "ask no more,
For it would be a sin." "Therefore,
335   His father said, "It must be so,
And since I see that you will go,
All you require we will provide.
May Jesus help you as you ride."[14]
"Dear Father," said Floris, "Then I'll say
340   What we will need upon the way.
For my own use you must provide
Seven fine horses in their pride,
And two with panniers that shall hold
A good supply of silver and gold,
345   And two with money that I may
Spend lavishly along the way,
And three with clothing rich and fine.
Please choose the best for me and mine.
Seven horses and men for me,
350   And in addition another three
Servants, and your own chamberlain,
For he's a man who can explain
Directions and aid us otherwise.
We'll all of us be in disguise
355   As wealthy merchants." Then the king
From the treasury had them bring
The golden cup that had been paid
For the purchasing of the maid,
And, "Use this, Floris," said the king,
360   "To pay, my son, for that sweet thing,
As the occasion may demand,
For Blancheflour of the gentle hand,
For Blancheflour, maiden fair of face."
Upon a palfrey[15] he had them place
365   A saddle, half as white as milk,

---

[14] This seems like a very Christian sentiment from a Saracen king!

[15] Palfrey: a riding horse, not one trained for war.

The other half as red as silk.
I can't tell all that saddle's beauty
(I must not pause; it's not my duty),
But wrought the saddlebow was with gold
370   And bands of orphrey[16] made to hold
The stones of power set therein.

Kind and courteous was the queen.
Glancing toward her lord the king,
Off her finger she drew a ring
375   And said to Floris, "Take this, dear,
And while you wear it, nothing fear:
Not burning fire, nor drowning sea,
Nor iron nor steel shall injure thee."[17]
He took his leave then to depart,
380   And sorrow lay in every heart.
His parents showed no greater joy
Than if in a grave were laid their boy.

Part II

THE JOURNEY

So Floris rides with a noble train,
And with them goes the chamberlain,
385   Down to the harbor. They begin
Their journey staying at the inn
Where Blancheflour that first night had stayed.
Expensively they are arrayed.
The gracious keeper of the inn
390   Sat Floris at the table's end
Upon the very nicest seat.
They all began to drink and eat
Except young Floris. He could not.
Upon Blancheflour was all his thought.

395   The innkeeper's wife, perceiving that
So deep in mourning Floris sat,
Said to her lord in a quiet voice,

---

[16]   Orphrey: an ornamental band woven of threads including gold (Old French *or*).

[17]   Lines 377–78 sound like a spell to accompany the magic ring.

"Good sir, now here is my advice:
Observe how he so sadly sits
400   That food and drink he quite forgets.
Little he eats and less he drinks.
That boy no merchant is, methinks."
To Floris quietly then said she,
"Full of mourning you seem to be.
405   The other day, exactly where
You're sitting sat Blancheflour the fair.
Hither was that maiden brought
By the merchants that had bought
The right to take her far from Spain
410   And sell her for a higher gain;
And you resemble her—I mean, her
Fine appearance and sad demeanor."
Floris listened to her with joy.
Never was there a gladder boy.
415   His heart began to lighten up,
And, having a servant fill his cup,
"Lady," he said, "this cup is thine,[18]
Both the vessel and the wine.
The wine and some good gold coins, too,
420   For speaking of her as you do.
Of her I think, for her I pine,
But I know not where I can find
My lady fair, though wind and rain
Shan't stop me searching far from Spain!"

425   Now Floris rested there that night
Till morning, when, at dawn's first light,
He set forth on the billowing sea.
Wind and weather favorably
Sped his ship till it came to land.
430   Floris thanked God upon the sand
For sending him where his lover was.
He thought he was in Paradise.

---

[18] Presumably this is not *the* cup, but just a casual fine goblet he uses for drinking.

IN BABYLON

Soon to Floris his servants told
The news that the amyral would hold
435   A feast where earls and barons too
Were all invited. Anyone who
Under that rulership held his land
Should honor him at his command.
Delighted at this, young Floris was
440   Planning to be a guest, because
He thought that once inside the hall
He'd see his love among them all.

When Floris came to the city fair,
He found an inn to lodge in there;
445   It was a palace, none its match.
The lord of that inn was very rich,
And he had traveled far and wide.
The child he sat down by his side
Upon the very nicest seat,
450   And all the guests began to eat,
And all who chose therein to dine
Made good cheer and drank good wine,
Eating and drinking all together.
But Floris's mind was on another;
455   So eat or drink, no, he could not,
For on Blancheflour was all his thought.
Then spoke the keeper of the inn,
Who was a noble, courteous man:
"Oh, child, I'm pleased you seem to be,
460   Taking such thought for my property."
"No, sir, of property I think not"
(For on Blancheflour was all his thought),
"For I have always on my mind
The merchandise I hope to find.
465   Yet it must also cause me woe,
For what I find, I must forgo."
Then spoke once more the lord of that inn:
"She sat the other day herein,
That lovely maiden Blancheflour.
470   Both in the hall and in the bower

She sat and mourned without an end
For her dear Floris, her life-long friend.
Never with joy or bliss contented,
Only for Floris she lamented."

475   Taking a cup with silver rim[19]
And scarlet cloak with miniver trim,
"Please," said Floris, "accept these, sir,
And for such gifts you may thank her.
Whoever could tell where they would take
480   That maiden, glad my heart would make."
"To Babylon she was conveyed,"
The burgess said. "The amyral paid
For that fair maiden, straight and bold,
Seven times her weight in gold,
485   Thinking, as soon as he had seen
The girl, to have her as his queen.
And then he placed her in his tower
Among the others with great honor."

Now Floris rested there that night
490   Until the morning at first light.
At early dawn he rose and dressed.
A hundred shillings Floris pressed
Upon his host. On leaving, he
Kissed host and hostess properly,
495   And asked the burgess if he would
Help him, in any way he could,
To win the maiden back, his love,
With any trick he might think of.
The host said, "Child, to a bridge you'll come,
500   And there you'll find the keeper home.
He lives down at the bridge's end.
A courtly man, he is my friend—
My brother, in fact; we've plighted troth.[20]
He can advise and guide you, both.
505   So take to him this ring from me
To indicate it's proper he

---

[19] Yet another precious cup, and again evidently not the special one.

[20] Observe that troth-plighting can confer honorary brotherhood. These men are not kin, but they each assume the privilege and responsibility of brothers.

Should help you, both in hall and bower,
As he would me, with all his power."
Unable to sit and be content,
510   Floris now took the ring and went,
And by the time the sun was high,
He to that bridge was drawing nigh.
Then Floris greeted with a kiss
The keeper of the bridge, Darrys,
515   And to the man he handed over
The ring that would get him to his lover.
Then through the token of the ring,
Floris enjoyed fair banqueting
On fish and flesh and tender bread,
520   And splendid wine, both white and red.
But ever he sat there, sad and cold.
Thus did Darrys the child behold.
"Dear child," he said, "what might this be,
That you so mournful here I see?
525   Is dislike of your dinner why
You look so sorrowful, and sigh?
Or do you just not like this inn?"
Then sweetly Floris answered him:
"Oh, sir, I've seldom, by God's grace,
530   Ever stayed in a better place.
May God let me await the day
When suitably I can repay!
But I have always on my mind
The merchandise I hope to find.
535   Yet it must also cause me woe,
For what I find, I must forgo."
"Child, will you tell me of your grief?
To help would please me beyond belief."
So every word to him he told
540   Of how that maiden had been sold,
And how he was son of a Spanish king,
Who a great love there did bring
To find some way—a trick—to win
His darling Blancheflour back again.

545 "Well, you're a dunce!" declared Darrys,
  And foolish he thinks young Floris is.
  "I know full well how it will go,
  For you desire to die, you know.
  The amyral calls to his tournaments
550 Some fifty kings; they have good sense,
  And none, not even the richest king,
  Would ever dare to do a thing
  Like this, for if the amyral knew,
  They would be slain—and so will you!
555 A wall encloses Babylon,
  The longest side sixteen miles long.
  Along the wall within each mile
  Are twenty-seven gates. Meanwhile,
  Inside, some twenty towers are
560 Guardians of the great bazaar
  Throughout the year. By day and night
  It's in full swing and quite a sight!
  Though every man who was ever born
  Upon his very life had sworn
565 To win that maiden fair and free,
  He'd surely die, and so will we.
  Beside the central square there stands
  A tower famous in many lands,
  And it's a hundred fathoms high.[21]
570 Whoever sees it, far or nigh,
  He must admit that we have here
  A tower without any peer.
  Of limestone and fine marble, there
  Is nothing like it anywhere.
575 Even the mortar's made so well
  That nothing breaks it, iron or steel.
  The finial on the roof with pride
  Was placed there so no one inside
  The walls or tower need ever bear
580 Either a torch or a lantern there,
  Because a globe is set thereon

---

[21] Fathom: about six feet. Could the poet be confusing this tower of Babylon with the tower of Babel?

That shines all night just like the sun.[22]
There is within that mighty tower
Many a noble lady's bower—
585   Some forty-two. It would be well
For any man therein to dwell!
He'd dare not dream of any bliss
Greater in all his life than this.
And servants there are in that place
590   To serve the maidens high of race,
But no man serves them in that tower
Who bears within his pants the power
To 'serve' the ladies, unless it happens
His parts are lacking, like a capon's.[23]
595   And at the gate there is a porter
Who is no fool and gives no quarter,
But wondrous proud is he withal,
And every day he wears rich pall.[24]

"The amyral has a custom, come,
600   So he has said, from Christendom.[25]
Each year he takes another wife
And loves the queen as his own life.
Each year they bring down from the tower
Every maiden from her bower,
605   And take her to an orchard where
No tree on earth is found more fair.
Therein is many a sweet bird's song.
A man might happily live there long.
Around the orchard is a wall
610   Of which the meanest stone of all
Is crystal. Therein a fountain flows
That anyone who sees it knows
Is no contrivance to despise:
Its waters flow from Paradise.
615   Its gravel is of gems, and it
Is magical, every precious bit.

---

[22] This is an example of an Oriental wonder. Similar gemstones working like streetlights are found in "Sir Orfeo" and "Sir Launfal," associated there with fairies.

[23] Capon: castrated rooster.

[24] An expensive fabric used for clothing.

[25] Possibly this is an allusion to the biblical story of Solomon's many wives and concubines.

This well inspires the greatest awe,
For if a woman breaks the law
And goes adulterous to the stream
620   And dips her hands to wash them clean,
Up boils the water in a flood
And then it turns as red as blood,
And she who makes the well turn red
Knows well that soon she will be dead.
625   But those who come there pure and clean
May safely wash their hands therein.
The water will stay calm and clear.
No danger from it need they fear.

"At the fountainhead stands a tree
630   The fairest that on earth may be,
And it is called the Tree of Love.
Flowers and blossoms bloom above,
And every virgin has to be
Brought there to stand beneath the tree.
635   If the first flower falls upon her,
She'll be queen with pomp and honor.
But if a maiden so special is
That the amyral wants her his,
The flower will land upon her hair
640   By magic.[26] Thus his lady fair
The amyral by the flower chooses—
And always on Blancheflour he gazes."

Three times Floris fainted when
He heard of what went on therein.
645   But he revived. He was not dead.
He wept and sorely sighed, and said,
"Darrys, now I shall surely die
Unless you help me." "Dear son, I
Only too well," he said, "can see
650   How much your trust is laid on me.
So here's the best advice I know.
I have no other. Tomorrow go

---

[26] This function of the amyral's magic tree makes us wonder. Is it real magic or a trick tree that he somehow controls, like the "Saracen magic" that created automatons and astrolabes and other clever devices so strange to Europeans?

With confidence to the tower here
As if you were an engineer.
655   Take square and scantilon[27] in your hand
Like any busy architect, and
Look at the tower, up and down.
The villainous porter, who is known
For fierceness, will come out to you
660   And ask what you intend to do,
And charge you with some felony,
The act of spying, probably.
Your answer should be very sweet.
Explain in manner mild and meek
665   That you're an engineer, and you,
Impressed by that tower, want to view
It close, to try to understand
How to build one in your own land.
Then very soon he will request
670   That you play him a game of chess,
And when you're playing chess with him,
Take care your purse is not too slim,
And you should always ready be
With twenty marks beside your knee.[28]
675   If you win anything of his,
Do not take much account of this,
But if he's winning, fair and square,
Make sure you have plenty of money there.
Thus you shall, with a trick, begin—
680   Since porters truly love to win—
To get him on your side this way.
Unless he helps you, no one may.
Then eagerly he'll ask you to
Come back so he can play with you.
685   You must agree. Be very nice,
And this time taking with you twice
As much. The third day, let him see
Your golden goblet casually,[29]
And give him large coins from your wallet

---

[27] Scantilon: carpenter's gauge.

[28] Marks: coins. Beside your knee: where the purse hangs.

[29] This is the third time we see a magnificent cup being bartered, and this time it does seem to
be *the* cup.

690   At every time he wants to call it.
         He'll ask you then, high on success,
         To wager your cup. Do not say yes.
         First of all you must yawn and say
         That you no longer want to play.
695   Thinking that it will bring him luck,
         He'll offer a lot. Then don't hold back:
         Give him the cup to have and hold,
         Though it be of the finest gold.
         He'll be so fond of you that he
700   Will bow to you and certainly
         Fall at your feet and be your man
         In every way he possibly can,
         And homage from him then you'll get,
         And he'll give you his hand on it."

705   Floris did all his friend Darrys
         Advised, and it turned out just like this.
         The porter was captured by the game,
         And Floris's man he soon became.
         The boy said, "Now, since you're my man,
710   You've got to help me all you can.
         I'll trust and open my heart to you.
         Advise me right, if you are true."
         Then every word to him he told
         Of how the maiden had been sold,
715   And how he was a prince of Spain
         Having come there for love, not gain,
         And hoped with trickery to win
         His darling Blancheflour back again.
         The porter sighed on hearing this,
720   And said, "I am betrayed, Floris,
         Through all your generosity.
         I'm worried about what I foresee,
         For I know what it's coming to:
         I'm sure to lose my life for you!
725   And yet I promise I shall not fail.
         So long as my two feet avail
         To walk on, I'll be true to all
         Your hopes, whatever may befall.
         So go on home now to your inn

730 And let me think how to begin.
    Between this time and three days hence
    I'll think up a plan that makes some sense."
    So Floris thanked him, yet upon
    His leaving, thought, *Three days? Too long!*

In the Tower

735 The porter thought of a strategy.
    Seeing flowers in a meadow, he
    Pretended it was the maiden's will
    And ordered picked two basketsful,
    And here was the perfect plan of his:
740 In one of the baskets he put Floris.
    The maidens who that basket bore
    Found it heavier than ever before
    And prayed for the porter an evil end,
    So many flowers he chose to send!
745 To Blancheflour he meant the girls to go.
    They went to another chamber, though.
    They should have gone to Blancheflour,
    But went to Claris's room next door.
    Cursing him for such trouble, they
750 Went home and let the basket stay.
    Claris, returning to her bower,
    Saw the basket and chose a flower.
    Then Floris, thinking it was his dear,
    Up in the basket leapt. In fear,
755 The startled maiden at once began
    To shriek, and cried out, "It's a man!"
    Floris saw it was not Blancheflour
    And down in the basket ducked once more.
    He thought he was lost as soon as seen,
760 But cared not for his life a bean!
    The maidens came in running then,
    A little group of eight or ten,
    And asked Claris what was the matter
    That she'd been making such a clatter.
765 Claris by now had guessed the basket
    Was for her friend, so when they asked it,
    Quick was the answer she replied

To all those maidens, saying, "I'd
Come to the basket"—this she told
770 The maidens—"better to behold
The flowers, and before I knew it,
Out darted a butterfly and flew at
My naked breast! So naturally
I screamed, and you all ran here to me."
775 The maidens laughed at her startlement
And, chuckling still, away they went.
As soon as they'd gone out the door,
Claris went quickly to Blancheflour
And said to her friend, "Please come and see
780 The beautiful flower that came to me.
I promise that you'll fancy it
After you've looked at it a bit."
"Go away, Claris," said Blancheflour.
"It's mean of you to mock me, for
785 They've told me that the amyral
Plans to wed me. He never shall!
The day will never come that he
Shall lay a husband's hand on me
Or that I'll ever be untrue
790 And change my love for someone new.
I'll not for love, and not for fear,
Forsake my Floris for someone here.
So much sweet Floris do I miss
That no one shall of me have bliss."
795 Claris stood there beholding both
Her tears and her empassioned troth,
And said, "My lady Blancheflour,
Now come with me to see that flower."
So then the lovely ladies two
800 Went to the basket, and Floris knew,
Having heard all, that it was she,
And up from the flowers again leapt he!

Pale went Blancheflour, changing hue
As each of them the other knew.
805 Without a word they ran together
And joyfully hugged and kissed each other.
Claris, patiently watching this,

Their loving expressions and their kiss,
Then said to her dear friend Blancheflour:
810 "So, you're acquainted with this flower?
A lady who knows such magic art
Should surely give her friend a part."
So now Blancheflour and her Floris,
Both sweet things, on hearing this,
815 Cried her mercy, and weeping they
Begged that she would not betray
Them to the king. "Doubt me no more,"
She said, "than were it *my* love, for
You must know plainly that I'm of
820 Your party, and will conceal your love."

Then to a bed the two were brought
With sheets of silken fabric wrought,
And there they drew themselves apart
And soon were talking heart to heart,
825 And no one could have then portrayed
The rejoicing those two lovers made.
Then Floris properly began
To pray: "Oh, Lord that created man,
For this I thank God's holy Son
830 That all my grief is past and done,
For now I've found my own sweet thing
And am released from sorrowing."
Claris all that they wanted served
Them secretly ... and not a word!

Discovery!

835 And now Claris of the lovely skin
Arose on the next morning, then
Called out to her good friend Blancheflour
To go with her up in the tower.
The girl said, "Coming now, Claris,"
840 But fell asleep as she answered this.
The amyral had a custom where,
On every day, a lovely pair
Of maidens from their private bower
Should serve him in the royal tower,

845   Bringing him water, cloth and basin
     For him to wash his hands and face in.
     One day would come two maidens fair,
     Then on the next another pair,
     But oftenest up in the tower
850   Would go Claris and fair Blancheflour.
     So when Claris now came alone,
     The amyral said, "But you're just one.
     Where is Blancheflour? There should be two.
     Why hasn't she come here with you?"

855   "Sir," she said (she was quick, all right!),
     "Blancheflour was wide awake all night.
     First she gazed, and then she wept,
     Read in her prayer book, never slept,
     Just prayed to God the whole night through
860   To shower blessings over you,
     And that He long your life should keep,
     And now the girl is fast asleep—
     So fast asleep, that maiden sweet,
     That she has not come up to greet
865   Her lord." "Now, truly," said the king,
     "Isn't she the sweetest thing!
     It's right I take her as my wife,
     Since she is praying for my life."
     Claris rose early another day
870   And Blancheflour barely woke to say
     "I'm coming," when Claris began
     To call her, and sound asleep again
     She fell, because she was so weary.
     Soon afterwards they'd all be sorry!

875   Now at the pillar[30] in the wall
     Claris filled up the golden bowl
     And once more called out to Blancheflour
     To come, then went up in the tower.

---

[30]   All four versions of the romance feature this pillar containing indoor plumbing, another
of the wonders of this Saracen palace. It is described most clearly in the Cambridge
manuscript, where Darrys explains, when first telling Floris about the tower, that a pillar
runs up through all the stories of the building, and within it water is conducted to each level
through a "pipe of bras" (Cambridge manuscript, line 225).

The amyral asked about Blancheflour:[31]
880 "Not up yet? What can the matter be?
She shows too little respect for me!"
He called his chamberlain, to say
That he must go down right away
To see why Blancheflour had not come
885 As formerly she would have done.

The chamberlain went forth and soon
He came into the maiden's room,
And in her bed, in an embrace,
He found the children face to face.
890 Together mouth to mouth they lay.
It did not take him long to say,
When up in the tower he ascended,
What he had seen. Greatly offended,
The amyral called for his sword, for he
895 Wanted to go himself to see.
He went to where the children were
And looked on sleeping Blancheflour.
He ordered then the covers cast
A little way below their breast,
900 And one was female, he found out,
The other male, beyond a doubt!

He quaked with anger where he stood
And very much was in the mood
To kill them both—but thought he'd stay
905 His hand till they had time to say
Just who they were, then he'd decide.
The children woke up terrified.
The sword above their heads they saw
And were afraid and much in awe.
910 Then Floris said to Blancheflour,
"There's no help for us any more,"
But begged the amyral nonetheless
To spare them. Tersely he told them, "Dress."
When they had gotten out of bed
915 And put some clothes on, he had them led

---

[31] This three-line sequence of the same rhyme is in the original; nothing has been omitted.

Outside, and both of them bound fast,
And into prison he had them cast.

He sent then for his barons, who
Would sit in judgment on the two.
920   And now each baron has left his home
And to the mighty tower come.
Then standing there among them all,
Angrily spoke the amyral:
"My lords, you've heard with what honor
925   I've treated the maiden Blancheflour,
How for her, standing straight and bold,
I gave seven times her weight in gold,
And thought, as soon as I had seen
The girl, to have her for my queen,
930   And placed her with the greatest honor
Among the maidens in my tower,
But to her bed I went, and when
I found a naked man therein,
The two so greatly did I loathe,
935   I very nearly slew them both.
They put me in a vengeful mood,
And yet I tempered my hot blood
Until you came. By your decree
This council should get revenge for me.
940   So now that everybody knows
My tale, avenge me on my foes!"

Up then spoke a king of the land:
"We've heard, and though we understand
Your point of view, before we find
945   A verdict, let us, if you don't mind,
See them and hear what they have to say,
In case there is anything to weigh
Against this. It's not valid yet
Until the accusation's met.
950   Without that, judgment in this case is
Lacking any legal basis."
So for the pair the amyral sent,
Though burning them was his firm intent.
Two servants went to bring the pair

955   To their death sentence. Weeping there,
Sorrowfully did the children go,
And each bemoaned the other's woe.

Floris said first to Blancheflour,
"There's no help for us any more.
960   If nature would let me survive
One death, I'd twice be burnt alive,
First for myself then you, you see,
Since you are doomed because of me."
And then Blancheflour replied, "Why, no.
965   Mine is the guilt for all our woe."
The boy took off the ring his mother
Gave him, handing it to his lover:
"Take this ring now, sweetheart mine.
You shall not die while it is thine."
970   But Blancheflour said, "Not so, my friend,
That's not how this affair will end—
By having this ring help only me
While forced your horrible death to see."
So she, when he handed her the ring,
975   Returned it quick as anything.
Neither wanting the other to die,
It fell between them. They let it lie
There on the floor. Along came a king
Who into his keeping took the ring.
980   The children, brought from their dungeon room,
Came out to the fire and certain doom.

Before the assembly they were brought,
And sad they both were in their thought.
So grim a nobleman was there none
985   In all that crowd who looked upon
Those children and would not willingly
Have cast his vote to set them free,
Or with his gold redeemed them there,
If such a gesture he could dare,
990   For Floris was such a fair youngling
And Blancheflour such a pretty thing.
But no man knew another's feeling.
Such mild thoughts no one was revealing.

The furious amyral could not
995   Cool down his blood—it was too hot.
He bade the children be brought along
And cast immediately upon
The fire. But then the noble king
Whispered how he'd found the ring,
1000   And how each wanted the other to live,
And how they'd argued, trying to give
It to each other. The amyral,
Wanting to hear more, had him call
The children back. He asked about
1005   The name of the boy, and found it out.
Then, "If you please, sir," Floris said,
"You cannot wish the maiden dead.
Good sir, instead of her, kill me
And let the little maiden be."
1010   Blancheflour said, at the very same time,
"The guilt for our deeds is only mine."
Enraged, the amyral made reply:
"Well, then, indeed, you both shall die!"
He drew his sword out from its sheath,
1015   Intent on putting the pair to death,
And Blancheflour stretched out her neck,
But Floris made her draw it back.
"I am the man, so I," he said,
"Go first! You may not first be dead."
1020   And Floris then put out his neck,
But Blancheflour made him draw it back.
"We must regret, sir," said the good king,
"Seeing these children arguing."

And then he who had found the ring
1025   Spoke on until he made them bring
The verdict "not guilty." To prevent
The children's death, he quickly went
To the amyral: "Sir, it's little worth
To sentence children to their death,
1030   And more worthwhile it's bound to be
To find from Floris by whom he
Was taught the trick that gave him power
To penetrate into your tower,

And who it was that brought him there.
1035   Informed thus, you can take more care."
The amyral said, "As God me save,
If Floris tells who was the knave
That taught him, I shall let him live."
"Never," said Floris, "unless you forgive
1040   My clever tutor along with me."
They all advised the amyral that he
Forgive both traitors their trespass
If Floris would tell them how it was.
So everything to them Floris told,
1045   How the maiden for him was sold,
How he, a prince, had left his home
In Spain and for love hither come
To try with trickery to win
His darling Blancheflour back again,
1050   And how the porter, willing or not,
Became his man, and how he got
The maidens to carry, by his craft,
Floris in flowers. And everyone laughed.

And now the amyral, bless his heart,
1055   Sat Floris by his side, apart.
And then he made him stand upright
And dubbed the boy, right there, a knight,
And said that henceforth he would be
The number one in his company.
1060   Then Floris, falling at his feet,
Begged him to free Blancheflour the sweet.
The amyral gave him his darling then,
And everyone thanked him once again.
He had them brought to a church, I'm told,
1065   To marry there with a ring of gold.
Then at his feet the children fell
To beg another boon as well,
And on the advice of Blancheflour
Claris was fetched down from the tower.
1070   The amyral took her as his queen,
And then a glorious feast was seen,
And never was food, I understand,
More rich and delicious in that land.

Not long after that party came
1075 Tidings to Floris from his home
That now the king his father was dead.
Then this is what the barons said:
He should go home and take the name
Of ruler, and his kingdom claim.
1080 The couple went to the amyral
To say goodbye. "Remain," was all
He said. But Floris with royal array
Went home and was crowned within a day.

[This "total resolution" in marriage and kingship, while
certainly abrupt, appropriately concludes the Egerton
version of the romance. The Cambridge Manuscript ends
with Floris giving wealth to everyone who has helped him,
followed by the usual benediction, lacking in Egerton.
The Auchinleck Manuscript has the couple becoming
Christian after returning home to Spain, and it too
concludes with a benediction.]

Two Additional Tales

1. Sir Libeaus and the Lamia

The story of the Loathly Lady takes many forms in medieval romance, though the enchanted lady rarely takes the shape of a lamia (snake-lady) or dragon, as here. These stanzas are from the last part of the romance *Lybeaus Desconus*, "The Fair Unknown," composed by Thomas Chestre in the final quarter of the fourteenth century. Chaucer refers to this romance at the end of "Sir Thopas" and probably derived some elements from it for his parody. It is introduced here for several reasons: its humor, the colorful description of a dragon, the lady who takes hold of her destiny, and the connection of the transformation theme with "Gawain/ Or someone close of kin" (lines 2107–08).

This is the story so far: Maid Elene has come to Camelot in search of a knight who can rescue her mistress, the Lady Synadoun, held captive by the evil magician Mabon and his brother Yrayne. The quest is taken on by Sir Libeaus (pronounced li-BOWS) Desconus, called the Fair Unknown because the court is unaware that he is Sir Gawain's son. He fights his way through thick and thin for some 2,000 lines, trying to get to Mabon's castle, doing battle along the way with a Saracen giant who swears by Termagaunt like Sir Thopas's giant. At last he arrives at the castle, has a monumental fight with the magicians, and succeeds in slaying Mabon, but wounded Yrayne escapes and runs away. Exhausted Libeaus now sits down on a stone wall outside the castle, thinking the building is empty.

In the following modernization the unusual short lines are kept, but the twelve-line stanza form, rhyming roughly aaXbbXccXddX, has been reduced to a more manageable six-line stanza, rhyming aaXbbX. Line numbers refer to the text of the Lambeth manuscript of this romance as edited by Maldwyn Mills for the Early English Text Society.

Sir Libeaus and the Lamia

He sat down on a wall
And nearby in the hall
    A window was unlatched.
Wonder at this event
2065   Gripped his heart, and sent
    It pounding as he watched.

Out came a serpent's head
With woman's face. It said,
    "Young am I, not old."
2070   Her wings and body blazed
All over, as he gazed,
    With fiery red and gold.

Her tail was very long,
Her feathers grim and strong.
2075   Listen now, and learn.
Libeaus began to sweat
As she slithered out
    The window, began to turn.

He was so terrified,
2080   He very nearly died.
    She coiled. He hoped she'd miss him.
Before he was aware
That it was coming, square
    Upon the mouth she kissed him!

2085   And when this kiss was over,
Her wings and tail and cover
    Of snake-skin fell away
And she emerged a human.
She was the fairest woman
2090   He'd seen in many a day.

But she was standing there
As the good Lord made her: bare.
    Ignoring the knight's distress,

"Libeaus," she said, "I owe

2095   You much for slaying my foe.
                    God give you all success.

"Just now you have slain two
Famous magicians, who
          Enchanted through the devil.
2100   To east, west, north and south,
Each cast spells from his mouth
          For injury and evil.

"Through spells they made me take
The shape of a giant snake,
2105   And, sadly, in that skin
Bound must I remain
Until I kissed Gawain
          Or someone close of kin.

"Because I am alive,
2110   All of my fifty-five
          Castles I give to you,
And with no parleying
We'll marry, if good King
          Arthur permits us to."

2115   Libeaus was glad indeed!
He leapt upon his steed,
          And left her standing there ...

[Since Sir Libeaus has not yet actually killed both wicked magicians, he is worried about the surviving brother ("Sore he dreaded Yrayne," line 2118), so off he rides—not to finish the job, as any reader or listener might expect, but instead to obtain for the Lady Synadoun, for she is naked, some clothes! Then they go to her nearest palace and have a seven-day-long party, after which they ride to Camelot where King Arthur grants the lady to Libeaus for his wife. This is followed by another party, forty days long, to celebrate the marriage, and somehow the other wicked magician is simply forgotten in the romance, as Libeaus and Lady Synadoun live happily ever after: "Now Jesus Christ our savior/ And his mother, that sweet flower,/ Grant us a good ending. Amen."]

most unfamiliar words in Scots dialect glossed.[3] For further information about this interesting ballad and closely related stories, Abigail Acland's website "Tam Lin" (http://tam-lin.org/) is highly recommended, as are Child's extensive introduction and notes. A melody for singing the ballad follows the text.

---

[3] The online *Dictionary of the Scots Language* at <http://www.dsl.ac.uk/dsl/index.html> has been useful for this task.

2. Tam Lin

According to Francis J. Child, the first recorded refe
Lin," ballad 39 (Versions A–I) in his collection, occ
1500s (Child I 336), the period of the late romanc
below was communicated by Robert Burns, and the tradi
was added soon after. Though clearly a ballad and not a mec
"Tam Lin" has such an affinity with the latter genre that it
this book. Many commentators, including Child (I 339), refe
"Tam Lin" has in common with "Thomas of Erceldoune," the
the fairy's taking of her lover-victim followed by the dange
sacrificed to Hell, the fairy hunt and their milk-white steeds
and following, and even the danger of sleeping under a tree
stanzas 26–27).[1] There is one remarkable difference from that
others, however: the protagonist is a mortal woman, Janet of
who saves Tam Lin from both fairyland and Hell.

With what appears to be intent, Janet goes to Carterh
(a real place not far from Selkirk in Scotland) and plucks a
calling forth Tam Lin, the guardian of the woods,[2] who gets
This does not seem to be a rape, although he is known to take
against their will. Nevertheless, her resulting pregnancy plac
awkward position at home in her father's hall, where she cla
dently believes, that she has been made pregnant by an elf mar
ness" that reveals her pregnancy, mentioned in stanza 10, is fi
sickness; we would describe her as pale. When she returns to
Woods, Janet calls forth Tam Lin again, this time discovering
human as herself—evidently a baptized Christian, therefore n
showing concern about her pregnancy, he tells her of his dange
and how to save him from it, a challenge that she valiantly und
shape-shifting that ensues reminds one of similar sequences in
(Child finds the theme running back to Greek and Cretan ta
ballad concludes with the Fairy Queen wishing that she had
Lin's eyes, a theme also encountered in "Sir Launfal."

The text given below, the most familiar of several versi
directly from Child's *English and Scottish Traditional Balla*

---

[1] Katharine Briggs in her *Dictionary of British Folk-Tales*, 4 vols. (Bloomingt
1970–71) declares that "this ballad is a compendium of Scottish folklore belie
of these (I 502).

[2] The plucked flower that calls forth the guardian is a common folklore theme,
familiar from "Beauty and the Beast."

Tam Lin

1.
O I forbid you, maidens a',
   That wear gowd[4] on your hair,
To come or gae by Carterhaugh,
   For young Tam Lin is there.

2.
There's nane that gaes by Carterhaugh
   But they leave him a wad,[5]
Either their rings, or green mantles,
   Or else their maidenhead.

3.
Janet has kilted her green kirtle[6]
   A little aboon[7] her knee,
And she has broded her yellow hair
   A little aboon her bree,[8]
And she's awa to Carterhaugh
   As fast as she can hie.

4.
When she came to Carterhaugh
   Tam Lin was at the well,
And there she fand his steed standing,
   But away was himsel.

5.
She had na pu'd a double rose,
   A rose but only twa,[9]
Till upon then started young Tam Lin,
   Says, "Lady, thou's pu nae mae.[10]

---

4   Gowd: gold.
5   Wad: offering.
6   Kirtle: skirt, dress.
7   Aboon: above.
8   Bree: brow.
9   Twa: two.
10 Thou's pu nae mae: you must pull (i.e., pluck) no more.

6. "Why pu's thou the rose, Janet,
        And why breaks thou the wand?"[11]
    Or why comes thou to Carterhaugh
        Withoutten my command?"

7. "Carterhaugh, it is my own,
        My daddy gave it me,
    I'll come and gang by Carterhaugh,
        And ask nae leave at thee."

8. Janet has kilted her green kirtle
        A little aboon her knee,
    And she has broded her yellow hair
        A little aboon her bree,
    And she is to her father's ha,[12]
        As fast as she can hie.

9. Four and twenty ladies fair
        Were playing at the ba,[13]
    And out then came the fair Janet,
        The flower among them a'.

10. Four and twenty ladies fair
        Were playing at the chess,
    And out then came the fair Janet,
        As green as onie glass.

11. Out then spake an auld grey knight,
        Lay oer the castle wa,
    And says, "Alas, fair Janet, for thee,
        But we'll be blamed a'."

12. "Haud[14] your tongue, ye auld fac'd knight,
        Some ill death may ye die!
    Father my bairn[15] on whom I will,
        I'll father none on thee."

---

11 Wand: stem.
12 Ha: hall.
13 Ba: ball.
14 Haud: hold.
15 Bairn: child's.

13.   Out then spak her father dear,
            And he spak meek and mild,
        "And ever alas, sweet Janet," he says,
            "I think thou gaest wi child."

14.   "If that I gae wi child, father,
            Mysel maun[16] bear the blame,
        There's neer[17] a laird about your ha,
            Shall get the bairn's name.

15.   "If my love were an earthly knight,
            As he's an elfin grey,
        I wad na gie[18] my ain true-love
            For nae lord that ye hae.

16.   "The steed that my true love rides on
            Is lighter than the wind,
        Wi siller[19] he is shod before,
            Wi burning gowd behind."

17.   Janet has kilted her green kirtle
            A little aboon her knee,
        And she has broded her yellow hair
            A little aboon her bree,
        And she's awa to Carterhaugh
            As fast as she can hie.

18.   When she came to Carterhaugh,
            Tam Lin was at the well,
        And there she fand his steed standing,
            But away was himsel.

19.   She had na pu'd a double rose,
            A rose but only twa,
        Till up then started young Tam Lin,
            Says, "Lady, thou pu's nae mae.

---

[16] Maun: must.

[17] Neer: never (i.e., not any).

[18] Wad na gie: would not give.

[19] Siller: silver.

20.   "Why pu's thou the rose, Janet,
  Amang the groves sae green,
 And a' to kill the bonny babe
  That we gat us between?"[20]

21.   "O tell me, tell me, Tam Lin," she says,
  "For's sake that died on tree,[21]
 If eer ye was in holy chapel,
  Or Christendom did see?"

22.   "Roxburgh he was my grandfather,[22]
  Took me with him to bide,
 And ance it fell upon a day
  That wae did me betide.[23]

23.   "And ance it fell upon a day
  A cauld day and a snell,[24]
 When we were frae the hunting come,
  That frae my horse I fell,
 The Queen o' Fairies she caught me,
  In yon green hill to dwell.

24.   "And pleasant is the fairy land,
  But, an eerie tale to tell,
 Ay at the end of seven years,
  We pay a tiend[25] to hell,
 I am sae fair and fu o flesh,
  I'm feard it be mysel.

---

[20] He appears to think that Janet is concocting an herbal abortifacient, and his response to this is to take full responsibility for his share in her pregnancy. Ignoring his concerned question, she moves quickly to the crucial matter of his nature, human or fairy.

[21] Tree: the Cross.

[22] Roxburgh: a town in the Scottish Borders near Kelso. Tam Lin's phrasing suggests that his grandfather was earl there.

[23] Wae did me betide: a woeful thing befell me.

[24] Snell: brisk.

[25] Tiend: tithe (tenth).

25.   "But the night is Halloween, lady,
        The morn is Hallowday,
    Then win me, win me, an ye will,
        For weel I wat[26] ye may.

26.   "Just at the mirk[27] and midnight hour
        The fairy folk will ride,
    And they that wad their true-love win,
        At Miles Cross they maun bide."

27.   "But how shall I thee ken,[28] Tam Lin,
        Or how my true-love know,
    Amang sa mony unco[29] knights,
        The like I never saw?"

28.   "O first let pass the black, lady,
        And syne[30] let pass the brown,
    But quickly run to the milk-white steed,
        Pu ye his rider down.

29.   "For I'll ride on the milk-white steed,
        And ay nearest the town,
    Because I was an earthly knight
        They gie me that renown.

30.   "My right hand will be gloved, lady,
        My left hand will be bare,
    Cockt up shall my bonnet be,
    And kaimed[31] down shall my hair,
        And thae's the takens I gie thee,
        Nae doubt I will be there.

---

[26] Weel I wat: well I know.

[27] Mirk: dark.

[28] Ken: recognize.

[29] Unco: unfamiliar.

[30] Syne: then.

[31] Kaimed: combed.

31.   "They'll turn me in your arms, lady,
            Into an esk and adder,[32]
        But hold me fast, and fear me not,
            I am your bairn's father.

32.   "They'll turn me to a bear sae grim,
            And then a lion bold,
        But hold me fast, and fear me not,
            As ye shall love your child.

33.   "Again they'll turn me in your arms
            To a red het gand of airn,[33]
        But hold me fast, and fear me not,
            I'll do to you nae harm.

34.   "And last they'll turn me in your arms
            Into the burning gleed,[34]
        Then throw me into well water,
            O throw me in with speed.

35.   "And then I'll be your ain true-love,
            I'll turn a naked knight,
        Then cover me wi your green mantle,
            And hide me out o sight."

36.   Gloomy, gloomy was the night,
            And eerie was the way,
        As fair Jenny in her green mantle
            To Miles Cross she did gae.

37.   At the mirk and midnight hour
            She heard the bridles ring,
        This lady was as glad at that
            As any earthly thing.

---

[32] Esk and adder: snakes.

[33] Red het gand of airn: red-hot piece of iron.

[34] Gleed: coal.

38.   First she let the black pass by,
                    And syne she let the brown,
          But quickly she ran to the milk-white steed,
                    And pu'd the rider down.

39.   Sae weel she minded what he did say,
                    And young Tam Lin did win,
          Syne covered him wi her green mantle,
                    As blythe's a bird in spring.

40.   Out then spak the Queen o Fairies,
                    Out of a bush o broom,
         "Them that has gotten young Tam Lin
                    Has gotten a stately groom."

41.   Out then spak the Queen o Fairies,
                    And an angry woman was she,
         "Shame betide her ill-far'd[35] face,
                    And an ill death may she die,
         For she's taen awa[36] the bonniest knight
                    In a' my companie.

42.   "But had I kend,[37] Tam Lin," she says,
                    "What now this night I see,
         I wad hae taen out thy twa grey een,[38]
                    And put in twa een o tree."[39]

---

[35] Ill-far'd: hostile.

[36] Taen awa: taken away.

[37] Kend: known.

[38] Een: eyes.

[39] Tree: wood.

A Singable Melody for "Tam Lin"[40]

O ... I forbid you, maidens a'/ That wear goud on your hair/ To Come or gae by Carterhaugh,/ For young Tam Lin is there.

---

[40] This melody is based on *The Songs of Robert Burns: Now First Printed with the Melodies for Which They Were Written, A Study in Tone-Poetry*, ed. James C. Dick (London: Henry Frowde, 1903), 328. It is annotated "Scots Musical Museum, 1796."

Hearing the Music of the Text

A Justification for Translating Metrical Romances into Verse

> *Writing of any kind fixes the word outside time, and silences it. The written word is a shadow. Shadows are silent. The reader breathes back life into that unmortality, and maybe noise into that silence.*
> —Ursula K. Le Guin, "Text, Silence, Performance"[1]

Offering here a justification for the translation of these metrical (i.e., rhythmic) romances into verse rather than prose, and a brief description of method, I begin with a fact. Poetic rhythms are physical, a throbbing felt in the body, projected by the "noise" of the words

---

[1]   *Dancing at the Edge of the World* (New York: Grove Press, 1989), 180.

(Le Guin's term), and emphasized by their chiming.[2] This physicality is the initial premise from which my practice proceeds, a fact so obvious that almost no one writing about poetry in modern times mentions it, or more likely they never even think of it.[3] To further elaborate this concept in simple but technical terms, the semantic or meaning structures of a poem (medieval or modern) are interlocked with the surface structure as displayed in its rhyme and meter, so that at the same time as the meanings are aimed at the mind, the rhythms marked by rhyme inscribe them on the body and the air around it.[4] The rhythms of the metrical romances in this book are especially pronounced, as the name of their genre indicates; and to ignore them would be to ignore the genre, to betray the hard-working rhymers who have made the choice to tell their stories in this form, and to deflate the liveliness and even the meaning of their stories—to reduce their bright "noise" to shadows. Therefore, in order to offer tales at all analogous to the originals, I feel that as translator I am obliged to give attention both to the meaning of the words and, so far as I am able, to the sound of the way

---

[2] Rhyme, whether word-initial alliteration (of sound, not letters as the term implies) or word-final chiming (rhyme as usually spoken of), is used in both Anglo-Saxon and modern poetry to mark and emphasize rhythm (meter as usually spoken of), though it has other uses as well. When referring to meter in the metrical romances, the combination of rhyme with recurrent rhythms will be assumed here, and the word "meter" itself pertains to the repeated patterns or rhythms of sound as in a song, rather than to the kinds of formal systems that can be specified by numerical terms, such as "iambic pentameter."

[3] While a brief appendix on translation practice is not the place to examine this subject in any depth, more must be said here since the physical aspect of meter is so important to my project. There are many phonological studies of the "noise" language makes when expressed aloud, endless formal discussions of the traditionally defined meters of high-culture poetry, and more recently some fine analyses of voicing texts (such as Gina Bloom, *Voice in Motion: Staging Gender, Shaping Sound in Early Modern England* [Philadelphia: U of Pennsylvania P, 2007]), but the physical and neurological aspect of meter itself has received little attention in modern times, and modern poets often dismiss regular metric patterns contemptuously as empty formalism or even as a "straitjacket" (a term used often). Yet the impact on the body of such rhythms is incontrovertible, and it follows clearly that they will also impact the mind. An excellent brief introduction to this line of thought is Derek Attridge's article "Rhythms in English Poetry" in *New Literary History* 4 (1990): 1015–38 (see also his book of a similar title); and two other scholars with an interest in this aspect of poetry are Amittai Aviram, *Telling Rhythm: Body and Meaning in Poetry* (Ann Arbor: U of Michigan P, 1994) and Joseph Tate, "Numme Feete: Meter in Early Modern England," *Early Modern Literary Studies* 7.1 (May 2001): 1–31. Tate observes of his Early Modern sources that "many of the period's rhetorical manuals, private letters, book prefaces and academic treatises affirm the importance of meter as both an aurally and physically affecting phenomenological experience and a crucial participant in the ideologically-bound codes signaling the economic, moral, and racial status of both subjects and objects, for better or worse" (1).

[4] "Rhythm in poetry is to the body and to physical reality as images are to social, language-mediated constructs" (Aviram 239).

they are strung together, the way the syntax winds through the constraints of the medieval poet's chosen meter.

On the premise, therefore, that this medieval dance of language is both performative and somatic, to be experienced along with the narrative, or rather, through which the narrative is to be experienced, my intent is to allow the modern reader to enjoy it this way also, to hear the story rippling through the drum-music of the meter.[5] My procedure then is as follows: After choosing the story, or having it choose me as is often the case, I find the edition of the Middle English text that best suits my purpose, and with my chosen edition at my side, or perhaps more than one, I do a rough, literal, line-by-line translation, trying to make the meaning of each line clear to myself. This sometimes means moving elements between lines to make them grammatical in modern English. From there, with the aid of a thesaurus and other props and always referring back to the medieval text, I "transpose" my rough translation into verse (not poetry in our modern elevated sense, but easy, rhymed story-telling). Being somewhat more obsessive about rhyming than medieval versifiers were, I tend to work toward rhymes more exact than theirs, though I often use slant rhyme as they do. Slant rhyme matches consonants but allows for assonant vowels, like ek/spak in "Sir Launfal" at lines 901 and 902, and like my own frequent said/maid in the same romance. Alternatively, slant rhyme may keep the vowel sounds but allow flexibility in the consonants, as in my "home/shone" rhyme in lines 933 and 936 of "Sir Launfal."[6] Sometimes, however, one simply has to resign oneself to more casual effects, as the medieval rhymers do frequently and with less anxiety. I should observe that in a serious bind they often throw all constraints to the wind, even giving up verse and going into prose. Aware of a more demanding audience, I do try harder to stick to the formal verse structure established in the romance, but the reader should be aware that rhyming must necessarily compromise sense to some degree,

---

5   Even though the medieval assumption seems to be that a romance was to be experienced orally (see Joyce Coleman, *Public Reading and the Reading Public in Late Medieval England and France* [Cambridge: Cambridge UP, 1996]), these modern translations can be enjoyed in silence, performed only in the head. They profit, however, from being read or performed aloud in order to hear, embodied, the music the language makes.

6   This particular example introduces another variable: the different pronunciations of American and British English. The o sounds of "home" and "shone" are nearly identical in American English, but in British English the more open o in "shone" would rhyme better with "John." "Rain" and "again" are close rhymes in British English but not American, and "was" and "laws" is closer in American English than in British. I especially enjoy and occasionally find useful such sound play as Chaucer's rhyming of one word with two words, usually with the verb "is": agoon is/onis, wyvys/alyve is ("Wife of Bath's Prologue," lines 9–10 and 39–40). My two-word rhymes are usually of the "mister/kissed her" kind, and they tend to be amusing in modern English.

or sticking rigorously to the sense will compromise rhyme, however desperately one tries to retain both elements.

In any case, the reader should not expect "poetry" in the high-culture sense.[7] The metrical romances are the popular culture of the late middle ages, and, unlike that paragon of medieval romance, *Sir Gawain and the Green Knight*, none of the nine romances here is complex. This is fluid story-telling in verse that may be appreciated on its own terms, and if it is found difficult, either it was confusing in the original and I have not sufficiently clarified what I understand the poet to mean, or else it was clear enough but I have simply failed to render it properly. This does not mean that there are no depths to explore in the material. Like any popular genre, romance expresses the dreams and anxieties and unacknowledged biases of the tellers and their audience.

When I said above that I "transpose" my rough translation, I was using that verb advisedly, because with so many words being the same or similar then and now, the experience of putting the Middle English of these metrical romances into modern English rhymes, while keeping the meter as intact as possible, seems to me more like transposing the melody of a familiar song between two different keys in music than like translating between two different languages. The nature of the task is different from translation between languages, as the words we share control straying from meaning in a way that a more alien vocabulary will not. When the "transposition" works, when the new sounds running through the metrical lines established by the medieval poet amazingly merge into meaningful sense, the experience is joyous, like striking the right note or chord for the key one is in. This rightness is also reassuring, for the dependable meters that accompany us through these nine romances aid in our trust as we watch the imperiled protagonists attempt to prevail in their world of strangeness.

My thesis here, to sum it up, is that poetry, whether lowbrow or high, should not only be seen on the page and thought about in the mind, but also felt and heard as an event for the body. The struggle to hold these stories to their "bodily" form has been a challenge and a delight, and I hope this joy of the rhythm and rhyming shines through, or chimes through, for the receptive reader. As Le Guin asserts in her book on writing, *Steering*

---

7   Sophisticated modern poets often eschew effects like rhyme and formal metrical patterns, or use these sparingly or skew them, arguing that the traditional forms when used today encourage banality. (One could compare the effects they seek with the innovative methods in music introduced by the Second Viennese School of Schoenberg, Berg, and Webern, and other "atonalities" that defy classical European musical forms.) Modern balladry, on the other hand, has affinities with the meters of medieval romance.

the Craft, "The sound of the language is where it all begins and what it all comes back to. The basic elements of the language are physical."[8]

―――――――――――

[8]   Le Guin, *Steering the Craft* (Portland, OR: The Eighth Mountain Press, 1998), 19.

BIBLIOGRAPHY

I. Medieval and Other Primary Sources Cited

Amadas and Ydoine. Trans. Ross G. Arthur. New York: Garland, 1993.

Blunden, Edmund, ed. *John Keats: Selected Poems.* London: Collins, 1955.

Bronson, Bertrand Harris. *The Traditional Tunes of the Child Ballads with Their Texts, According to the Extant Records of Great Britain and North America.* 4 vols. Princeton and Berkeley: Princeton UP and U of California P, 1959.

Burns, Robert. *The Songs of Robert Burns: Now First Printed with the Melodies for Which They Were Written, A Study in Tone-Poetry.* Ed. James C. Dick. London: Henry Frowde, 1903.

Chaucer, Geoffrey. *The Canterbury Tales Complete.* Ed. Larry D. Benson. Boston: Houghton Mifflin Co., 2000.

——. *The Canterbury Tales: A Facsimile and Transcription of the Hengwrt Manuscript*. Ed. Paul Ruggiers. Norman: U of Oklahoma P, 1979.

Chestre, Thomas. *Sir Launfal*. Ed. A.J. Bliss. London: Nelson, 1960.

Child, Francis James. *The English and Scottish Popular Ballads*. 5 vols. New York: Dover, 1965.

Dante Alighieri. *The Purgatorio*. Trans. John Ciardi. New York: New American Library, 1957.

Gower, John. *Confessio Amantis*. <http://etext.lib.virginia.edu/toc/modeng/public/GowConf.html>.

Henryson, Robert. "The Tale of Orpheus and Euridices his Quene." *Selected Poems*. Ed. W.R.J. Barron. Manchester: Fyfield Books, 1981. 92–109.

Lang, Andrew. "Aucassin and Nicolette" (retold). In Loomis, *Medieval Romances*, 242–83.

Laskaya, Anne, and Eve Salisbury. *The Middle English Breton Lays*. Kalamazoo: TEAMS/Western Michigan UP, 2001.

Loomis, Roger Sherman, and Laura Hibbard Loomis, eds. *Medieval Romances*. New York: Modern Library, 1957. (Contains Andrew Lang's retelling of "Aucassin and Nicolette.")

Lybeaus Desconus. Ed. Maldwyn Mills. Early English Text Society No. 261. Oxford: Oxford UP, 1969.

Mills, Maldwyn, ed. *Six Middle English Romances*. London: Dent, 1973. (Contains "Sir Gowther.")

The Romance and Prophecies of Thomas of Erceldoune. Ed. J.A.H. Murray. Early English Text Society No. 61. London: N. Trübner, 1875.

Sir Launfal. See Chestre, Thomas.

Sir Orfeo. Ed. A.J. Bliss. Oxford: Oxford UP, 1954.

"The Sowdone of Babylon" (The Sultan of Babylon). Ed. Alan Lupack. *Three Middle English Charlemagne Romances*. Kalamazoo: TEAMS/Western Michigan UP, 1990. Also at <http://www.lib. rochester.edu/camelot/teams/sultfrm.htm>.

Stevick, Robert D. *Five Middle English Narratives*. Indianapolis: The Bobbs-Merrill Company, 1967. (Contains "Floris and Blancheflour.")

Virgil. *The Georgics*. Book 4 (containing the story of Orpheus). <http:// www.sacred-texts.com/cla/virgil/geo/geo104.htm>.

The Wallace: Selections. Ed. Anne McKim for TEAMS Middle English Texts. <http://www.lib.rochester.edu/camelot/teams/wallfrm.htm>.

Ydoine and Amadas. Trans. Ross G. Arthur. <http://www.yorku.ca/inpar/ amadas_arthur.pdf>.

II. Secondary Texts Cited

Acland, Abigail. "Tam Lin" (website). <http://tam-lin.org/>.

Allen, Dorena. "Orpheus and Orfeo: The Dead and the *Taken*." *Medium Aevum* 33 (1964): 102–11.

Archibald, Elizabeth. *Incest and the Medieval Imagination*. Oxford: Clarendon Press, 2001.

Attridge, Derek. "Rhythms in English Poetry." *New Literary History* 4 (1990): 1015–38.

Aviram, Amittai. *Telling Rhythm: Body and Meaning in Poetry*. Ann Arbor: U of Michigan P, 1994.

Barnes, Geraldine. *Counsel and Strategy in Middle English Romance*. Cambridge: Brewer, 1993.

Barron, W.R.J. *English Medieval Romance*. London: Longman, 1987.

Beidler, Peter G., ed. *The Wife of Bath*. Boston: Bedford/St. Martin's, 1996.

Bloom, Gina. *Voice in Motion: Staging Gender, Shaping Sound in Early Modern England*. Philadelphia: U of Pennsylvania P, 2007.

Briggs, Katharine, ed. *A Dictionary of British Folk-Tales in the English Language*. 4 vols. Bloomington: Indiana UP, 1970–71.

Burkert, Walter. *Homo Necans: The Anthropology of Ancient Greek Sacrificial Ritual and Myths*. Trans. Peter Bing. Berkeley: U of California P, 1983.

Cassell's French-English, English-French Dictionary. New York: Funk & Wagnalls Company, 1951.

Cohen, Jeffrey Jerome. "Gowther Among the Dogs: Becoming Human c. 1400." *Becoming Male in the Middle Ages*. Ed. Jeffrey Jerome Cohen and Bonnie Wheeler. New York: Garland, 1997. 219–44.

——, ed. *Of Giants: Sex, Monsters, and the Middle Ages*. Minneapolis: U of Minnesota P, 1999.

Coleman, Joyce. *Public Reading and the Reading Public in Late Medieval England and France*. Cambridge: Cambridge UP, 1996.

Cooper, Helen. *The English Romance in Time: Transforming Motifs from Geoffrey of Monmouth to the Death of Shakespeare*. Oxford: Oxford UP, 2004.

Dictionary of the Scots Language. <http://www.dsl.ac.uk/dsl/index.html>.

Eisner, Sigmund. *A Tale of Wonder: A Source Study of The Wife of Bath's Tale*. Folcroft, PA: Folcroft Press, 1970.

Fisher, John Hurt. *John Gower: Moral Philosopher and Friend of Chaucer*. London: Methuen, 1965.

Frye, Northrop. *The Secular Scripture: A Study of the Structure of Romance*. Cambridge, MA: Harvard UP, 1976.

Gerritson, Willem P., and Anthony G. van Melle. *Dictionary of Medieval Heroes*. Woodbridge, Suffolk: Boydell Press, 1998.

Gough, A.B. "The Constance Saga." *Palaestra* 23 (1902): 1–84.

Green, Richard Firth. *A Crisis of Truth: Law and Literature in Ricardian England*. Philadelphia: U of Pennsylvania P, 1999.

Hahn, Thomas. "Gawain and Popular Romance in Britain," *The Cambridge Companion to Medieval Romance*. Cambridge: UP, 2000. 218–36.

——. "Old Wives' Tales and Masculine Identities," *Retelling Tales: Essays in Honor of Russell Peck*. Ed. Thomas Hahn and Alan Lupack. Cambridge: D.S. Brewer, 1997. 91–108.

Henderson, Lizanne, and Edward J. Cowan. *Scottish Fairy Belief: A History*. East Linton, Scotland: Tuckwell Press, 2001.

Hope-Moncrief, A.R. *The Romance of Chivalry*. North Hollywood, CA: Newcastle Publishing Co., 1976.

Le Guin, Ursula K. *Steering the Craft: Essays and Discussions on Story Writing*. Portland, OR: The Eighth Mountain Press, 1998.

——. *Dancing at the Edge of the World*. New York: Grove Press, 1989.

Leodhas, Sorche Nic. *Thistle and Thyme: Tales and Legends from Scotland*. New York: Holt Rinehart and Winston, 1962.

Levertov, Denise. *Relearning the Alphabet*. New York: New Directions, 1970.

Lewis, C.S. *The Discarded Image: An Introduction to Medieval and Renaissance Literature*. Cambridge: Cambridge UP, 1964.

Lindahl, Carl. "The Oral Undertones of Late Medieval Romance." *Oral Tradition in the Middle Ages*. Ed. W.F.H. Nicolaisen. New York: Medieval & Renaissance Texts & Studies, 1995. 59–75.

Loomis, Laura Hubbard. "Sir Thopas." *Sources and Analogues of the Canterbury Tales*. Ed. W.F. Bryan and Germaine Dempster. New York: Humanities Press, 1958. 486–559.

Metlitski, Dorothee. *The Matter of Araby in Medieval England*. New Haven: Yale UP, 1977.

Osborn, Marijane. *Romancing the Goddess: Three Middle English Romances About Women.* Urbana: University of Illinois Press, 1998.

The Oxford Dictionary of Saints. Ed. David Hugh Farmer. Oxford: Clarendon Press, 1978.

Patterson, Lee. *Temporal Circumstances: Form and History in the Canterbury Tales.* New York: Palgrave Macmillan, 2006.

Peck, Russell A. "Folklore and Powerful Women in Gower's 'Tale of Florent.'" *The English "Loathly Lady" Tales: Boundaries, Traditions, Motifs.* Ed. S. Elizabeth Pasmore and Susan Carter. Studies in Medieval Culture XLVIII. Kalamazoo: Medieval Institute Publications, 2007. 100–45.

Ramey, Lynn Tarte. *Christian, Saracen and Genre in Medieval French Literature.* New York: Routledge, 2001.

Rice, Joanne A. *Middle English Romance: An Annotated Bibliography, 1955–1985.* New York: Garland, 1987.

Rickert, Edith. "The Old English Offa Saga." *Modern Philology* 2 (1904): 29–76; *Modern Philology* 3 (1905): 321–79.

Schlauch, Margaret. *Chaucer's Constance and Accused Queens.* New York: Columbia UP, 1927.

Severs, J. Burke. *A Manual of the Writings in Middle English, 1050–1500, I. Romances.* New Haven: Connecticut Academy of Arts and Sciences, 1967.

Stratmann, Francis Henry. *A Middle-English Dictionary.* A New Edition by Henry Bradley. Oxford: Oxford UP, 1891.

Tate, Joseph. "Numme Feete: Meter in Early Modern England." *Early Modern Literary Studies* 7.1 (May 2001): 1–31.

Teale, Sarah. *Giants.* New York: Abrams, 1979.

Whetter, K.S. *Understanding Genre and Medieval Romance.* Aldershot, UK: Ashgate, 2008.

INDEX

PRELIMINARY NOTE:

Glosses of words in individual romances are not included in this index, nor, on the whole, are details or themes within the texts that are not commented upon in the footnotes. Details in substantive footnotes are included.

From the Publisher

A name never says it all, but the word "Broadview" expresses a good deal of the philosophy behind our company. We are open to a broad range of academic approaches and political viewpoints. We pay attention to the broad impact book publishing and book printing has in the wider world; for some years now we have used 100% recycled paper for most titles. Our publishing program is internationally oriented and broad-ranging. Our individual titles often appeal to a broad readership too; many are of interest as much to general readers as to academics and students.

Founded in 1985, Broadview remains a fully independent company owned by its shareholders—not an imprint or subsidiary of a larger multinational.

For the most accurate information on our books (including information on pricing, editions, and formats) please visit our website at www.broadviewpress.com. Our print books and ebooks are also available for sale on our site.

broadview press
www.broadviewpress.com

This book is made of paper from well-managed FSC® - certified
forests, recycled materials, and other controlled sources.